Angels and Economists

Will B. Misquoted

Printed in the United States of America

Second Edition, 2020

ISBN-13: 978-0-9994189-1-8

Will.B.Misquoted@gmail.com

Table of Contents

Introduction

Economics is the study of the production, distribution, and consumption of goods and services in a world where resources are scarce. The area that houses these activities is known as an *economy*. We *economists* (people who study economics) use theories developed from observing the outcomes of economic activities to advise people on the impact that changes in public policy would have on consumers and businesses. It is ultimately up to the citizens and their politicians to use our advice to determine how they want to operate their economy to achieve their production, distribution, and consumption goals. Unfortunately, economists are usually ignored. And the facts/conclusions we present are bastardized by the people who do not like what the science of economics has to say about the effects of public programs aimed at addressing poverty and inequality (e.g., providing government welfare). Economists find themselves in this position because they point out that, despite

1

noble intentions, these popular programs do not deliver positive long-term results.

Adherents to the *science of economics (positive economics)* have yet to fully accept the age-old lesson that using sober logic instead of compassionate emotion is a tactless move when discussing any controversial subject with the general public. The angry backlash a person experiences while communicating ghastly economic principles, when presenting the logical conclusions of seemingly benevolent statements like:

"Anybody that works full-time should be able to have a middle-class lifestyle."

"We need to provide government benefits to those who cannot help themselves."

"The government needs to redistribute profit to improve the standard of living for every member of society."

"Everybody deserves to go to college."

"The government should make it easier to own a home."

—is caused by their stubbornness in refusing to blindly go along with socially acceptable *economic opinions* (*normative economics*). The public naively believes that if the intention behind a policy is good, positive results will follow. If you're smart, you should avoid conflict and go along with this philosophy and leave the consequences that result from this simplistic way of thinking for others to worry about.

Since there are people in this world set on living the life of a social outcast by championing truth, I've written this book to respond to a few of the misguided socioeconomic narratives a person is likely to encounter from one's friends and family. My goal is to use a positive economic lens to provide insight into how economists view the impacts, on the poor and middle class, from popular economic policies that were created to increase prosperity and reduce inequality. Cause and effect logic will be used to support my critique of minimum wage laws, welfare programs, profit redistribution schemes, and subsidies.

Chapter 1: Minimum Wage

Topic 1: What is the Minimum Wage?

The minimum wage is the lowest hourly wage an employer can legally pay somebody to work for them. In the United States, the minimum wage gets set by federal, state, and local governments. With a few exceptions, any employer who pays their workers a rate less than the minimum wage is breaking the law. The government imposes this policy with the intention of increasing the income for the lowest-paid members of society. The federal minimum wage is currently set at $7.25 an hour [1]. To a caring American, minimum wage laws seem socially and morally responsible. However, the reality is that mandating employers increase the amount of money they pay their lowest skilled workers has consequences that people often overlook. To understand the negative impacts of the minimum wage laws, we have to first discuss how the *market (trade between buyers and sellers)* sets wages for minimum wage workers and then introduce an economic concept known as a *price floor*.

You've probably heard before that prices are determined by supply and demand. But what does that mean? Prices are set at the point where buyers and sellers agree to trade money for goods and services. From the buyer's point of view (demand side), they make purchases when they find a seller selling the products they want, at a price low enough for them to accept. From the seller's point of view (supply side), they sell items when a buyer offers them enough money to part with the goods or services they have for sale. A buyer is looking to maximize the amount of benefit they receive from a purchase while paying the least amount of money they can, and a seller is looking to get as much money as possible for the products they're selling. A trade happens when a buyer and seller can agree on a price.

Watch an episode of Pawn Stars on the History Channel, and you'll see an example of how prices get set in real-time. The sellers coming into the store are looking to receive as much money as they can for the items they're selling, while the burly store owners are trying to pay the least amount of money they can for those items. A deal happens when both sides settle on a price. You will also see sales not happening on the show because the buyer and seller can't reach an agreement. In a *free market (economy where trades are determined by buyers and sellers, with limited third party interference),* sales do not occur when the price is higher than what a buyer is willing to pay for a good or service, or if the price is too low for the seller to supply the good or service. The fact that people walk away from trades that they disagree with helps keep the price expectations of buyers and sellers in line with *market prices (the average prices other buyers and sellers are settling on for similar goods)*.

Prices are set a little differently for mass-produced goods. It would be impossible for producers and consumers to haggle on all the products being traded for a ready-made product like a box of wine (please reserve your judgement). Therefore, both parties have to communicate via the number of purchases/sales made at different price points. Producers will raise their prices if their products are selling well, and they will reduce their prices if their products are selling poorly. On the other hand, consumers will purchase more of an item when prices are low and pull back on their purchases as the prices rise.

An ongoing trade occurs when individuals work for a business. The service being sold is the labor from the worker, the worker is the supplier, and the company is the buyer. Like every other good or service being bought and sold, the market determines the price and quantity of labor traded via supply and demand. The worker lets the business know how much money they will accept to supply the business with their work. On the other side of the table, the company tells the worker how much they're willing to pay for their labor. If they can settle on a price, just like in our Pawn Stars example above, then the worker gets paid money by the employer, and the business receives labor from the worker. If they cannot agree on a price, the worker stays unemployed, and the company doesn't receive any work from that worker.

Now that we have briefly explained how the market sets prices via supply and demand, let's talk about what happens when people choose to interfere with the market price via *price floors. A price floor is the lowest price a person can legally sell a particular item.* For example, if the government were to impose a $5 price floor regulation on a gallon of gas, it would be illegal for anybody to sell a gallon of gas for less than $5. The problem with price floors is that they interfere with buyers and sellers to determine the prices and quantities they are willing to buy/sell goods and services. Price floors cause fewer goods and services from being sold because they raise the prices for purchasers. Even if a supplier is willing to supply buyers with products at prices lower than the price floor the government sets, they cannot do it because selling at prices below the price floor will get them fined or banned from doing business. Going back to our gasoline example, if buyers and sellers are both willing to buy/sell a gallon of gas at a rate of $2.50, but a price floor of $5 per gallon is put in place by the government, fewer gallons of gas would be sold. The reason for the decrease in sales should be obvious. There will be fewer customers willing to pay $5.00 a gallon for gas than $2.50 a gallon, and the customers that do continue purchasing gas will purchase fewer gallons.

The minimum wage is the most well-known example of a price floor. If I were a worker with zero experience, I might be willing to work for $5 an hour to fold jeans at Abercrombie (other perks of the job include getting hit on by attractive women). And Abercrombie might be willing to offer me a job at $5 an hour. However, because there is a minimum wage in place, Abercrombie has to pay me at least $7.25 an hour to hire me legally. In that scenario, I might not get the job. Since Abercrombie has to pay its employees at least $7.25 an hour, they might only consider candidates with more experience/skills or employ fewer people. To reiterate, this is the biggest problem with the minimum wage—it forces higher prices on both parties in a transaction. Higher labor prices for the seller (worker) on the surface sounds like a good thing, which is why people advocate for the minimum wage. However, those higher labor prices result in less labor being purchased by employers, which means fewer jobs, and fewer work hours for minimum wage workers.

Imagine it's the end of the winter season, and a store has a lot of unsold sweaters. What will they do? Most people who have worked in retail or are savvy shoppers should know the answer to this. The store will sell their sweaters at discounted rates to quickly clear their inventory and generate revenue. It is an unchanging law of economics; if a good or service is offered for sale at a lower price, it will sell much quicker than if the price was higher. In other words, when sellers can't sell an item, they lower their prices to attract customers.

What does one do if they find themselves unemployed and having a tough time finding a job? Skilled workers lower the amount of money they're willing to accept for their next position to land a job as quickly as possible. The minimum wage law removes the ability of unskilled workers from doing the same thing. These workers cannot say to an employer, "I will work for $5.00 an hour if you hire me today." The minimum wage commands that workers charge their employers at least $7.25 an hour for their labor, eliminating their ability to lower the price they will accept to secure a job. Without the ability to negotiate wages below the set minimum wage, people with no/low skills have a much tougher time finding jobs. This situation ultimately limits opportunities to work and accumulate skills for those at the bottom of the job market.

Topic 2: Why do some workers have trouble earning more than the minimum wage?

You would probably agree that the vast majority of those earning minimum wages have little or no job skills. When I was a teenager with no experience, most employers valued an hour of my labor to be worth less than the minimum wage, as evidenced by the extreme difficulty I had in finding a job. However, like most Americans today, I am paid more than the minimum wage. What changed between the teenage me and the present me (besides the beer gut)? I acquired skills both on the job and through education. These new skills raised the demand that employers have for my labor. As a teenage employee, I used to stand around asking what mindless chore I should be completing for my supervisor. As a skilled employee, I add value to the companies I work for by independently completing numerous complex accounting/financial tasks and creating new procedures to decrease risk and increase profits for my employers. High demand for my labor increases the amount of money that employers are willing to pay me, and as I gained skills, the supply of workers who could perform the same type of work that I could shrank. A small number of alternative candidates for my employers to choose from means that employers will need to offer me higher pay if they want to be the employer I decide to work for. These are the supply and demand reasons for why income increases for workers when they gain relevant job skills. Let's explore how the laws of supply and demand set the wages for unskilled workers.

Supply and Demand explanations for why Inexperienced Workers Earn Less Money than Skilled Workers:

Supply:

Inexperienced workers tend to start out in jobs that require a very basic set of skills. In these jobs, employees usually perform a variety of simple tasks that can be mastered in a very short amount of time for any able-bodied person. Simply put, almost anybody can do these jobs. Since most people can be taught to perform a low-skilled job, there is a high supply of potential candidates who can perform minimum wage level work. In contrast, high-skilled jobs require workers that possess extensive experience and training to perform very specialized tasks. For example, almost 100% of the employees in my office building could roll up their sleeves, and with a few hours of training, be taught to work in the various functions of a retail or fast food environment.

On the other hand, it would be impossible to find enough fast-food workers in the country to replace all of the accountants and financial analysts in my company without years of training. I'm not suggesting that high-skilled workers are *innately* more skilled or have a larger intellect than the inexperienced workers in the scenario presented above. A topic typically glossed over when discussing pay discrepancies between low-skilled/high-skilled workers is the sweat equity that goes into earning higher incomes. High-skilled workers start as unskilled workers and have to acquire expertise in their fields over many years of work, education, and training.

In most cases, a higher percentage of "qualified workers" (i.e., workers that can perform the job) apply for a single minimum wage job opening, as opposed to a high-skilled job opening. Most of the minimum wage applicants are willing to accept low pay to land these jobs, as their lack of skills prevents them from securing higher-paid positions. The large supply of qualified unskilled candidates provides businesses with many options to choose from when deciding who to hire to perform menial tasks. The workers that ask for too much money are easily replaced with ones that will accept lower pay to do the same job. In contrast, there are far fewer qualified candidates available for jobs that require highly skilled labor. Employers have a much harder time securing skilled labor, and therefore have to offer more money to hire qualified candidates for jobs that require specialized expertise.

Demand:

Demand for labor is derived from the perceived value that employers receive from hiring a worker. An employer will generally hire somebody as long as they believe that they will receive more benefits from the employees' labor than the cost to employ them. Let's run through a quick scenario to highlight this concept.

Suppose we could get the government to raise the minimum wage to $15 an hour. If I, as an employer, believed that I would only be receiving $14 of value from hiring an additional employee (I'm not including administration, employee benefits, and payroll tax costs to keep things simple), I would immediately go on a hiring freeze. Why? Any new hires would be taking more resources away from my business than they would be adding. Facts and anecdotes show that unskilled workers don't contribute much of a monetary benefit for employers in their roles (not a moral judgment, just a business one). Unfortunately, the perceived value of labor can be tough to quantify, causing most people to overvalue what their skills are worth to an employer. In the following paragraphs, I'll demonstrate the difficulty of determining the value of low-skilled labor.

Let's go back to our fast food example— if there is only one cashier at a burger joint, and that burger joint makes $200 an hour by selling burgers, how much value as measured in dollars does that cashier add per hour to the business? I often ask this question to friends and family. Surprisingly, many of them believe that the cashier is contributing $200 an hour in value. That is why most of the people I know are not economists or accountants. Those answering the question failed to consider all the other inputs going into the sale of those burgers. Most of the time: the cashier does not cook the burger; they don't deliver the raw beef patties to the store; they don't slaughter the cow to make the beef patty; and they don't raise or feed the cow. A comparable amount of resources and labor goes into creating and assembling all the other ingredients that go into a burger (bun, cheese, lettuce, pickles, tomatoes, etc.). Finally, the cashier did not build and normally does not maintain the restaurant's equipment (other than routine cleanings). If we listed out all the people who had a hand in allowing the customer to purchase that burger, it would be as long as the credits at the end of a movie. The $200 an hour the burger joint earns is being distributed among all those participants. Returning to the cashier's contribution, they ring up orders and hand the customers their food. As a former cashier, I can attest that it's a very low-value function.

Going back to the original question, "How much value does the cashier add?", It would be almost impossible for most business owners to determine the exact value the cashier is adding to the business. Therefore, what the hiring managers do to determine how much they will pay their cashiers is to throw out a low-ball offer to their applicants. If none of their candidates agree to this wage, the employer will continue to increase the wages they're willing to pay. Up to a point where a qualified candidate accepts their offer, or until the cost makes it no longer profitable enough for them to hire a separate employee to run the cash register.

Why do inexperienced workers earn low pay? There is a large supply of people willing and able to do their jobs, and the demand for low-skilled workers is low because the function they perform doesn't add much in perceived value to the businesses they work for. Therefore, employers will not pay these workers much money since they are easily replaced with readily available alternatives. Those statements might sound harsh and insensitive to some, but economic truth, like truth in general, is ordinarily ugly.

Topic 3: Wouldn't employers just pay their employees pennies for their labor if there was no minimum wage?

A greedy employer might want to pay an employee nothing for their labor, but their greed is checked by the same market forces as every other customer— prices are determined by both supply and demand. For example, I might want (*demand*) to buy a boat for $1, but no one in their right mind will sell (*supply)* me a new or even slightly used boat at that price. I could try to recruit homeless people for landscaping work at $1 a day wages, and I guarantee that I'd hire no one. I can't make either of those deals happen because boat sellers can find somebody else that will offer them more than $1 for their boat, and a homeless person can make much more than a $1 a day begging. Having alternatives on the supply or demand side is just one way the market prevents one-sided trade from happening. The point is, employers might have a demand for free or underpriced labor, but people will refuse to supply them with work if they don't receive appropriate compensation for their services.

As an aside, proponents of the minimum wage often try to bring up unpaid internships as an example of people willing to work for free. However, they fail to mention the fantastic experience that interns receive from these positions. These training programs drastically increase students' ability to land a job after graduation and increase their potential earnings. The opportunities and skills interns receive serve as their compensation. Let us not forget about all the interns that owe their fame and fortune to their internships (an intern with the initials M.L. comes to mind).

Let's explore the question of how wages are set from a different angle. If the minimum wage law is the only thing preventing employers from paying their employees little to nothing to work for them, why do only 3.9% of American workers earn minimum wages [1]? *Wouldn't 100% of employees be earning the minimum wage if minimum wage laws were the only measure preventing employers from underpaying their workers?* As stated before, I make more than the minimum wage.

Why is my employer paying me more than they legally have to? Why are employers all over America, paying 96.1% of working Americans a higher rate than the minimum wage? The answer: The American economy is set up as a "mostly" free market system that does not interfere with buyers and sellers to set prices. In a free market system, an employer can't force anybody to work for them. Workers have the power to choose the terms they're willing to accept from employers, to supply them with labor. Conversely, employees can't force employers to hire them if they make outrageous compensation demands relative to the value they are providing to the business.

The free market system's beauty is that if either side of the trade is unwilling to accept the other party's terms, the deal never happens. Free markets maintain the sensibility of employers and employees when negotiating employment agreements. In this system, employers must compete with each other for labor. Workers will go to the bidders that offer them the best overall package regarding compensation, future opportunity, location, work environment/schedule, access to business relationships, culture, etc. As workers gain and sharpen their skills, more employers will come and bid up the price of their labor. Low-skilled workers earn low wages because there aren't any bidders willing to pay high prices for their work.

To illustrate my point about the effects of having alternatives in the market, let's look at my employment situation and ask the following question: what would I do if my boss were to inform me that the company will be lowering my salary down to the minimum wage? Apart from giving him a customary cursing, I'd quit and send out my resume to other companies. The point is, the company I work for has no way to keep me if they offer a total compensation package that is much lower than what I could receive at other employers for similar work. Like every other seasoned worker, the skills I have acquired while suffering through the drudgery of work and attending school has a value that employers are willing to pay for. Workers can quickly determine what their skills are worth in the labor market by

23

looking at the offers other employers are making to workers with similar skills and experience. Luckily, in our expanding digital world, people can do this with a few swift clicks of the mouse.

Switching gears. Let's suppose every employer in the country was to meet and somehow force the government to abolish the minimum wage. They also collectively agree not to pay any of their employees more than $1 a day. Even with these changes, they still couldn't obtain labor at this rate. Why? No one in our wealthy country will work for any employer for $1 a day unless they get compensated in other ways. People would naturally gravitate towards better alternatives. What is most likely to happen is people would quit their jobs, sleep in, and spend time with their families. They would barter and trade amongst themselves, to acquire the goods and services they need to survive. Any business determined to pay their employees $1 a day will go bankrupt because they will not attract any workers to continue their operations.

In the case of setting wages, the only way to break the laws of supply and demand is with force. If businesses were determined to use governments to acquire cheap labor, the government would have to legalize kidnapping to bring workers to retail locations, factories, and offices. This hypothetical system would also require the lawful use of violence to extract labor from those who are rounded up. In a nutshell, slavery would need to be legalized to control wages effectively.

With every purchase, regardless of whether it's a boat or labor, economics's unshakeable law remains the same—Supply and Demand will determine the price. A high supply of unskilled workers, and low demand for their labor, will result in lower pay. Whereas, a small supply of high-skilled workers, and a high demand for their work, will yield higher wages. The key to getting higher compensation is to gain specialized skills that employers will pay for. The best avenues to start building skills for a person with no skills are working in low paid jobs or getting a useful education.

Topic 4: *Will raising the minimum wage help the poor?*

There are positive and negative aspects associated with every government policy. With the minimum wage, the primary benefit is an increased hourly wage rate for unskilled workers. Supporters of the minimum wage focus on touting this benefit while completely dismissing the negative consequences. Regarding the costs, when minimum wage laws are implemented/raised, employers will slash staff, cut hours, automate tasks, raise prices, and eliminate some/all of their operations. Why? They have limited resources to produce their goods and services. If they don't control their prices and production costs, they'll be unable to continue providing their products to their customers.

The primary cost of a minimum wage law is the reduction in the number of jobs and work hours for low-skilled workers. Labor is like any other good or service that people purchase in their daily life; the quantities bought and sold are affected by prices. If a business charges more for beer, the parties you attend will be less fun because the people throwing them will commit the sin of purchasing fewer beers. *All else equal, buyers will buy less when items cost more.* Companies and consumers do not have unlimited resources. They have to react to rising prices by reducing their purchases and looking for cheaper alternatives, or they'll go broke. Naturally, a business will buy less unskilled labor when that cost increases. The long-term consequence for a society with fewer minimum wage jobs is a delay in skills development for young workers. The result is that there are workers in their 20's with limited skills employed in jobs typically performed by teenagers in the past.

The secondary cost of a minimum wage law is that it results in businesses raising the prices they charge their customers. Producers will try to pass back as much of the increased costs of employing inexperienced workers as they can to consumers. In response to these price increases, customers will pull back on their purchases of items heavily impacted by the minimum wage, culminating in businesses slashing production of the goods and services that are no longer profitable to produce. The reason it's rare to see full-service gas stations is because it's not cost-effective for gas stations to employ people to pump gas at minimum wage prices.

Lastly, as an aside, wealthy people do not face the same consequences as poor people due to a minimum wage law. Most high-income earners' income remains unchanged when the government mandates a minimum wage increase unless they directly employ minimum wage workers. When the prices at the grocery store increase to cover the costs associated with minimum wage hikes, rich folks won't have to decrease consumption as much as the poorer members of society because they are better equipped to afford these increases.

To sum it up— Minimum wage laws decimate the poor by; reducing their ability to find employers willing to hire them or give them more hours in their shifts, delaying their ability to accumulate skills, and raising their prices for the daily essentials.

For those reasons, economists believe that the costs of implementing minimum wage laws far outweigh the benefits of a higher wage rate.

Topic 5: Why doesn't the unemployment rate increase much when the minimum wage is raised?

Elementary school math can answer the question, "Why the unemployment rate doesn't increase dramatically when the minimum wage is raised?". There aren't that many people who work for minimum wages—only 3.9% of American workers earn the minimum wage, according to the Bureau of Labor Statistics [1]. The rest of the working population makes more. Using that information, we can deduce that *if every worker earning minimum wages lost their job due to a minimum wage hike, the unemployment rate would only rise by 3.9%.*

Doing some simple math, let's say a minimum wage increase of $2 an hour causes the unemployment rate among those currently earning the minimum wage to rise by 20% (completely hypothetical). The situation would be disastrous for low-skilled workers. But if we calculate the *overall* unemployment rate (the statistic normally reported by mainstream media outlets), the unemployment rate would only increase by a whopping 0.78%! (That's right simple elementary math - 100% x 3.9% x 20% = 0.78%). You will not read or hear any breaking news stories on how the unemployment rate increased by less than 1%, but 20% of jobs will have disappeared for those at the very bottom of the labor force! Also, the job losses would be under-reported if employers were planning to hire more unskilled workers before the reveal of a minimum wage hike.

The second reason that the overall unemployment rate doesn't rise much when minimum wages are raised is that the reported unemployment rates are skewed by the statistical model that determines who is unemployed. The official unemployment rate is not based on the number of able-bodied Americans who are out of work. The unemployment rate only takes into account the number of Americans who are out of work and who have actively searched for a job within the past four weeks. Those without a job AND not seeking employment are neither "employed" nor "unemployed"; they are quietly swept under the rug and considered out of the labor force [2]. Let's use this information to anecdotally explore why the unemployment rate is not an accurate metric to measure the job losses among low-skilled workers when the minimum wage is raised.

A large number of unskilled workers are usually young, with very few financial obligations. They're probably not looking for jobs like their next meal depends on it. From my first-hand experience, most young people are insecure and tend to avoid rejection like the plague. It doesn't take many "No's" from employers to get young workers to stop applying for jobs. Therefore, large numbers from this group can go uncounted as officially unemployed. In high school, my friends and I would periodically complete job applications at various companies. We were usually turned down because we had no experience and offered no real immediate skills or benefits to the businesses we were applying to. Moreover, the employers would be forced to pay us minimum wages if they did hire us. These rejections often led to discouragement and stopped us from actively seeking work. We were by our own definitions unemployed; however, since most of the time during this period, we had not put out applications in the prior four weeks, we would not be counted in the "official unemployment numbers."

The best way of tracking the job losses caused by the minimum wage is to focus on the unemployment numbers for groups that possess no/low skills since these are the individuals most likely to be earning these wages. Teenagers are a group that economists would expect to be low-skilled because it is unlikely the average teenager has been working long enough to have accumulated many job skills. As expected, after analyzing past unemployment rates among teenagers, we see increased unemployment for this group after minimum wages are raised [10]. Unfortunately, the only people who tend to track and discuss the specific unemployment demographics of workers are old and boring economists like me.

To recap, the two reasons that the *overall* unemployment rate doesn't increase much when the minimum wage is hiked are:

1. Minimum wages don't affect most of the working population.

2. Many of the unskilled workers who lose out on job opportunities are not counted due to how the official unemployment rate is calculated.

The reason economists know that job losses occur due to the minimum wage is that, even though the data is incomplete, the unemployment rate in specific groups we would expect to earn minimum wages rise when the minimum wage is increased [10]. And also, basic economics tells us that price floors cause fewer goods and services to be sold.

Topic 6: How is somebody supposed to live off of the minimum wage?

I earned minimum wage once, and I'm willing to bet that more than half of you reading this book made it as well at some point in your working life. The majority of us former and current minimum wage earners are still alive and kicking, despite the claim from many, "a person can't live off of the minimum wage." The point of that statement from minimum wage supporters is, "a person can't live *independently or comfortably* off of a minimum wage income." I completely agree with that. It would be challenging to finance an apartment, cover your utilities, and pay for groceries on a minimum wage paycheck. Unfortunately, the hard truth is there is no perfect solution to this problem.

Society has two options when it comes to the minimum wage:

Have a minimum wage: This will raise the pay of unskilled workers who can get a job and maintain their work hours. As a consequence of this action, there will be fewer job opportunities/reduced hours for low-skilled workers as a whole.

Abolish the minimum wage: This will result in wages for unskilled labor getting priced at levels low enough to entice employers to hire workers with limited job experience. Minimum wage workers will have to deal with a period of meager pay until they collect the skills to raise their incomes.

Given a choice between these two bad options, economists like myself believe that the course of action that has a better chance of decreasing systemic poverty is choosing the path with no minimum wage. The reason? The job losses associated with minimum wages cause long term poverty because it stunts the development of skills among low-skilled workers. Whereas, having an economy with no minimum wage, and as a result, more jobs for people with low skills, would provide workers with more opportunities to build up their skills to land higher-paying positions.

People seem to forget that earning minimum wages only covers a short time in most people's careers. That's why only 3.9% of workers earn minimum wage at any given time, but the bulk of able-bodied Americans have worked for minimum wage or less at some point in their lives. This nostalgic exercise serves (not to remind you of the awful burger flipping or table waiting) to demonstrate how quickly people enter the workforce earning the minimum wage and then transition into making higher pay as they gain more skills. If that weren't true, the percentage of minimum wage workers would be much higher than 3.9%. Typically, what I have seen with people in my own life is a transition to a higher paying role as early as 3-6 months after starting a minimum wage position.

For those wondering how people survive during periods of earning low wages, the following resources are where most minimum wage workers turn to to make ends meet:

1. Family - This is probably the first place most people get help while working at a minimum wage job. A person's family usually offers food, shelter, and additional support if they can. My family is where I obtained financial help when I earned minimum wages working at a grocery store. Not everybody has this option, so we have to talk about alternatives for the family.

2. Friends - This is typically the second place people go to for help while working at their minimum wage job. Usually, this help comes in the form of a place to crash or living with a few roommates to split the bills. Friends are also a valuable resource to get information about which companies are

hiring workers with similar experience levels to your own and what skills to pursue to land a higher paying job.

3. The Community – There are always citizens in the community who will offer great advice on obtaining the resources needed to survive during the lean periods and what one needs to do to be successful—those who are struggling need to put themselves out there and ask for help. Countless non-profit charities offer free hot meals, shelter, groceries, health clinics, career advisement centers, daycare, and housing, to name a few. Most charities will almost always have enough resources to care for the genuinely needy. I've volunteered at many different organizations over the years. In my experience, I can assure you that anybody willing to accept charity for assistance will receive the help they need to survive. Despite the long wait times at these facilities, everyone leaves with food in their stomachs. Also, there are always members of the community willing to provide others

with job information. I have directed a few struggling grads to employment opportunities at companies I've worked for in the past, and I've received more than my fair share of career advice from neighbors and strangers alike.

5. Welfare Programs- Welfare programs are assistance programs run by the government that provides food, shelter, and money to qualified applicants. We will discuss the problems with welfare later in this book.

Topic 7: Wouldn't a higher minimum wage improve the economy since minimum wage workers would have more money to spend on goods and services?

Supporters of the minimum wage often make the argument, "A higher minimum wage would allow unskilled workers to spend more money in the economy, thereby increasing the revenue for businesses, which would then allow employers to continue paying these higher wages." This cycle sounds like a win-win situation for both workers and employers. Unfortunately, as we've previously discussed, the minimum wage does not guarantee higher incomes for low-skilled workers. A society can have a $15 minimum wage on the books, but it doesn't mean anything if employers are unable or unwilling to pay for higher labor prices. Any increases in the minimum wage rate will be offset by reduced employment and slashed hours for workers earning the minimum wage. Proponents of the minimum wage frequently forget that the paycheck an hourly worker receives is a function of both the *wage rate* and the *number of work hours* purchased by an employer. For argument's sake, we will ignore the fact that employers will layoff workers in the face of rising minimum wages to examine the other adverse effects raising the minimum wage would have on the economy.

Let's assume that all of the employers in a fictional country called *Utopia* get together and agree to double their lowest-paid employees' wages. Also, the employers agree not to fire any of their staff or reduce their work hours. They call this new arrangement, *The Fair Agreement*. To understand if The Fair Agreement will lead to higher economic growth, we have to explore what happens to the production of goods and services after the unskilled workers receive their increased pay rate.

As we discussed earlier, the resources available to a business are not unlimited. The companies in Utopia that employ low-skilled workers will have to take the resources to pay for the increased wages from the company's purchase and maintenance of *capital* (*equipment used to produce/distribute goods and services*), their profits, and the salaries of their skilled workers. For now, we'll focus on the effects of cutting spending on capital.

Later in the book, we'll discuss why it would be hard if not

impossible to reduce the wages of skilled employees and why

cutting profits would result in businesses closing up shop.

When the labor costs increase for the Utopian employers,

they will be forced to cut their spending on maintaining factory

equipment, trucks, construction equipment, buildings, office

supplies, computers, electronic servers, and other capital. The use

of capital is the difference-maker when it comes to the

productivity rate of an economy. Even a slight reduction in the

amount of spending on capital will dramatically reduce the

productivity rate for workers, resulting in the Utopian economy

producing fewer goods and services. To understand why I say

productivity would quickly tank when businesses started cutting

back on buying/maintaining their capital: try cooking dinner

tonight without your stove, oven, or microwave; or attempt to

travel 30 miles in any direction without the use of a car, bus,

train, or bike. People would literally/figuratively live like animals

without the use of human-made capital. Unfortunately for

Utopian workers, a lower productivity rate will reduce the number of products available for them to purchase. This situation leads us to the question— Does a less productive economy, with more cash going to unskilled workers, help or hurt the poor?

If all a society had to do to create a higher standard of living was to give everyone more money, the treasury could add more zeroes to everybody's bank account and simply throw money out of planes. People often overlook the fact that money is just a tool that an economy uses to simplify trade, not the actual end product. Workers don't go to work to earn money just to stare at paper bills or numbers in their bank account. People go to work, so the goods and services they create can be traded for the merchandise and services that other people produce like: housing, food, or the healthcare services required to unclog arteries from years of bad diet and alcohol abuse. *The goods and services in an economy are what determines how well off the citizens are. Nobody is better off in a society that simply raises the amount of money that people are paid without increasing the number of goods and services produced.* Prices for consumer goods will rise

if a society pays their workers more money, without any

increases in the level of productivity. The phenomenon of rising

consumer prices is caused by the supply of money in an area of

the economy, increasing faster than the products available for

consumption. Consumers will have to offer more and more

dollars to producers to purchase the same items as the amount of

money continues to grow relative to the number of products in

the economy. In economics, we call this *inflation.*

The Results of the Fair Agreement are:

-Low-skilled workers in the Utopian economy would earn more

money once the minimum wage is raised. However, due to the

diminished productivity coming from workers with less access to

capital, there would be fewer goods and services available for

them to consume.

-More dollars being used for consumer goods, from the increases in wages, combined with the effect of fewer goods and services being manufactured, will jack up the prices for the item's consumer's purchase.

Will increasing the wages going to the low-skilled workers in Utopia provide these citizens with greater purchasing power, leading to increased economic activity? This economists' answer is a resounding, NO! The problem the Utopian economy would experience from artificially raising the price of labor via higher minimum wage mandates is decreased productivity from reduced capital spending and inflation in consumer goods. Minimum wage hikes in the real-world economy would result in outcomes identical to the Utopian economy, with the added problem of employee layoffs.

The only way to increase the standard of living for everyone in an economy is to increase the amount of capital in the economy and increase their workers' skills to be able to use that capital effectively so that the economy produces a higher quantity/quality of goods and services. While the only way for an individual to raise their standard of living is to cultivate more skills so that their labor becomes more productive. Raising the minimum wage stunts the development of skills by reducing employment opportunities for unskilled workers and also decreases the amount of money that businesses have available to invest in capital goods— these actions make everyone just a little bit poorer.

Topic 8: Why does Costco pay their employees more money than Walmart for the same type of work?

Supporters of a higher minimum wage often point out, "Costco pays their retail employees more money than Walmart pays theirs." This statement is an attempt to show that employers can afford to pay their unskilled workers more money without any adverse effects. Their logic is that Costco and Walmart are both profitable companies that have comparable business models, and so both companies should pay their store employees similar wages. In actuality, the two retailers are very different in how they earn their money and conduct their day to day operations. Those who argue that Walmart and similar stores should pay their retail employees the same amount of money as Costco employees are paid are singling out one desirable aspect of how Costco operates (higher pay for workers). They rarely attempt to explore the differences in the business models that contribute to this variance in wages.

The following are just three quick examples of how Costco runs their stores differently from Walmart:

1. *Costco charges money for the right to shop at their stores*- In the United States, Costco charges a $55 annual membership fee for their cheapest membership (Gold Star). As of February 15, 2015, Costco had 44.6 million paid cardholders [3]. If you do the math on the membership fees, Costco earns billions of dollars just for allowing consumers to make purchases at their stores. Walmart stores (excluding Sam's Club) don't charge a membership fee, and therefore don't receive the same multibillion-dollar stream of revenue.

2. *Costco sells items in bulk*- Selling items in large quantities means that the revenue for most of Costco's transactions will be much higher than the transactions at

traditional retailers. Instead of selling a 4-pack of AA batteries, Costco is selling AA batteries in 24-packs.

As a side note, the bulk sales model allows Costco customers to save money on their household essentials. For most producers, it will usually cost less per unit to produce and sell goods in higher quantities than selling the same products in smaller amounts. Economists call these savings from bulk production *Economies of Scale*. In our personal lives, we see the concept of Economies of Scale at work when we cook large quantities of food. It takes less time, water, and electricity to cook a large pot of spaghetti and meatballs with four servings than to separately prepare each serving four different times. Costco and its suppliers are passing most of these savings down to their customers.

3. *Costco can use a warehouse-style store layout to sell*

goods- Costco doesn't need to stock shelves for most of the items they carry because their products are sold in large boxes that can be stacked on top of a pallet for customers to grab. Costco employees can simply use forklifts to drop off pallets stocked with goods to the store's various departments. On top of moving the pallets around the store, Walmart has to employ workers to remove the goods from the pallets and storage boxes and then line the items up individually on shelves. This difference means that Costco can use significantly less manual labor than Walmart to replenish their sales floor.

After analyzing the two operating models, it becomes apparent to this former retail worker that Costco's business requires different skills than Walmart's (e.g., ability to use an electric forklift, maintaining a warehouse sales floor, and anecdotally a higher caliber of customer service skills to keep their members happy). From a demand perspective, the Costco business model demands slightly higher-skilled labor for its operations. Also, Costco has the revenue from membership fees and bulk sales to afford the higher pay.

Let's imagine what would happen if the government forced Walmart and other retailers to adopt Costco's business model to raise the pay for all retail workers. I visited around 15 stores this week (Walmart, Target, Home Depot, various clothing retailers, among others). To mimic Costco's subscription business, I would have had to pay membership fees at every one of those stores. Doing this would add $825 (15 * 55 = $825) in fees every year, just to have the privilege of purchasing items from the stores I visited this week alone! Additionally, if every retail business adopted the Costco model, consumers would be required to buy everything in bulk. Instead of popping into the grocery store to purchase a single Greek yogurt after my workout, I would have to buy a pack of 18!

Even though they have drastically different business models, it makes everyone richer that both Costco and Walmart exist. The two stores provide consumers with a wide variety of purchasing options. I can save money by buying a two-year supply of batteries and other goods I prefer to purchase in bulk at Costco. On the other hand, at Walmart Stores, I have access to a more extensive selection of groceries and other items that I want to purchase in smaller quantities. Lastly, both businesses further contribute to the economy by employing countless people, from low-skilled workers in their retail operations — to higher-skilled workers like truck drivers, warehouse workers, procurement teams, back-office workers, sales and marketing professionals, accountants, etc.

***Topic 9: How is it fair that the CEO's of large
corporations take home millions of dollars a year
when low-skilled workers at the same companies are
struggling to get by?***

I often hear the outrage most people have over the fact that
high-skilled workers out-earn unskilled workers by ridiculous
margins. For a long time, I shared their anger. It doesn't *seem fair*
that some workers can earn so much while others earn so little—
however, the laws of supply and demand reign sovereign over the
prices of everything, including wages. Lowering the pay of
executives will not raise the income of low-skilled workers
because they are in entirely separate categories when it comes to
labor. An employer looking to hire somebody to clean their floors
does not consider the salary of the accountants working in their
building when determining what to pay for their new cleaning
personnel. Companies price out the wages they're willing to offer
minimum wage workers based on their demand for that particular
function and the supply of available candidates that can/will
perform that type of work. I will not justify or discuss the

morality of the high pay that executives and other highly skilled workers receive. My goal is to explain why the salary of high-skilled workers (executives in particular) is so high and why trying to lower executive pay via forceful mandates is easier said than done.

Like the rest of society's workers, the pay for top-level executives is set by supply and demand. In regards to the demand for these workers: hiring managers must decide how much they're willing to pay the executives they hire by determining what traits they require to fill their open positions (e.g., education, experience, skills, business connections, among others), and how much value those positions add to their company. On the supply-side: companies must evaluate the number of eligible candidates that best fit the description for the skills and experience required for the job and the alternative job prospects available to them. The dominant supply and demand reason for why executives earn so much money is: the *supply* of candidates who meet the rigorous standards of company leadership is often tiny because these organizations are *demanding* extraordinary resumes to fill their top-level positions. The result is vigorous competition among different companies to hire from a small pool of candidates. This competition leads to higher wages for executive workers as companies have to bid over one another to recruit and retain the executives likely to be the best performers.

Workers with executive skills and experience who are not offered competitive compensation/advancement opportunities will work for rival companies that make them a better proposal. High demand for their skills is why these workers don't quit their jobs and work at the burger joints close to their homes. The options available to a high-skilled worker will offer much higher benefits than the wages earned at a retail fast food position. The myriad of alternative employers aggressively competing to acquire executive-level candidates explains why companies in a free market can't low-ball this group of workers during the hiring process; and also why companies have to continue offering them increasing bonuses to keep them from being lured away by other employers.

One commonly proposed way to limit executive pay is through government-mandated income caps for executives. However, in response to such a move, most employees with executive skills and experience will merely exercise their options: some of them will retire; some will start their own companies to receive compensation as an owner and not as an employee; but in most situations, companies will begin to exploit "creative accounting maneuvers" to compensate high-level executives appropriately (e.g., deferred stock compensation, gifting, and good old-fashioned accounting fraud), to ensure that they can secure the valuable labor required to run their businesses from these highly skilled individuals.

Do executives deserve their high pay? The question of who deserves what is subjective and philosophical, not objective or scientific. The science of economics can only provide a descriptive explanation of economic situations and the resulting cause and effect of different actions. We economists are just offering our own subjective opinions when saying whether an economic activity is philosophically right or wrong. Asking an economist, "Is it fair for CEOs to earn so much money, while some employees at the same company earn so much less?" is akin to asking a physician: "Is it fair that childhood cancers are more aggressive than adult cancers?" Economists and physicians can only offer subjective answers when faced with these unanswerable questions. Objectively, economists and recruiters know that there is an incredibly high demand and an extremely low supply of ultra-high-skilled individuals, which requires companies to pay outrageous amounts of money to secure labor from this group of workers.

Topic 10: In this economy, where there are people with bachelor's and master's degrees taking minimum wage jobs, how can you argue that there is no need to raise the minimum wage?

I completely agree with the view, "there are too many people with advanced degrees working in minimum wage jobs." Is this a sign that an economy with a low minimum wage is only producing low paying jobs? Does the fact that there are people with degrees earning low wages contradict my repeated statements that increased skills will lead to higher pay? No. Why are so many well-educated people only able to find crappy low paying jobs? The answer is simple, take a close look at the education of people who have difficulty finding jobs that match their salary expectations.

A large number of college-educated workers that have difficulty securing decent-paying jobs are earning degrees in fields with horrible employment prospects: Fine Arts, English Literature, Music Therapy, Film, Dance, Anthropology, just to name a few. It's no mystery to any person who has a friend or family member earning low wages with an advanced degree why that individual is working a low paying job after college. They studied subjects that appealed to them without discovering and developing the skills employers demand and require for their job openings. Low employer demand for artists is why a person with a graphic design degree makes around $15 an hour if they are lucky enough to land a job [11]. High employer demand for computer programmers is why a competent person with a degree in computer engineering from a decent school earns about double what the graphic designer makes and is all but guaranteed a job after graduation [12].

Society should only start to panic about large numbers of highly-educated citizens being employed at crappy jobs when fast-food workers have degrees in subjects that are perpetually in demand – those in specific science, technology, engineering, or math (STEM) majors. If the reality were, "a large number of graduates with their bachelor's in engineering and computer programming from reputable schools are working at the local coffee shop," then it's time to panic. It should come as no surprise to anyone that the only thing most graphic designers are designing is a cappuccino.

Let's rephrase the concept of *skills* leading to high paying jobs. It's not about just having any old skill; it's about possessing and expertly wielding abilities that employers need to operate their businesses. It is difficult to sell a product or service that people don't want to buy. Employers just aren't interested in purchasing labor from college graduates with skill sets that don't add value to their company. Prospective college students need to start verifying for themselves that their college education will lead to a job before investing massive amounts of time, money, and energy in pursuing a particular field of study.

A family friend gave me the best piece of advice regarding how to properly choose a college major while I was only a junior in high school. She told me to spend a few hours searching through job boards to ensure that the jobs I wanted to pursue existed in large numbers in the areas I planned to live. She also told me to check the "job requirements" section to ensure employers would hire people with the degree I wanted to earn. One thing that astounds me about students today is the lack of time they spend thinking about the specifics of: how difficult it is to find a job with their intended major; which companies they're going to apply to; and how they are going to get the skills/experience that employers are listing as requirements on their job advertisements. The situation facing many graduates is perfectly captured by the old quote, "If you fail to plan, you're planning to fail."

Topic 11: Isn't it a problem that most people earning the minimum wage are adults?

According to the U.S. Bureau of Labor Statistics, approximately half of the workers earning the minimum wage are 24 years old or younger (this age group is labeled as **teenagers and young adults** by the statisticians). That means the other half of minimum wage earners are older than 24 (this age group is marked as **adults**) [1]. If that statistic were all you knew about minimum wage workers' demographics in the U.S., it would sound like a large percentage of American adults are trapped in minimum wage jobs. Let's put this figure into context by combining it with another minimum wage indicator that we've already discussed:

The minimum wage only affects about 4% of all American workers (~3.9%, refer to the section *"Wouldn't employers just pay employees pennies for their labor if there was no minimum wage?"*)

Approximately 50% of minimum wage earners are adults 24 or older.

These statistics indicate that only 2% of adult workers earn minimum wage (4% x 50% = 2%)! To provide further insight into the statistic that "half of the minimum wage workers are adults," we also need to discuss the importance of group sizes when comparing statistics between groups. A larger number of people can be categorized as adults than can be classified as teenagers and college students. Definitionally speaking, the period of being a young worker only covers 8 years of life (24–16 = 8), whereas the adult worker group can span 53 years or more (78–25 = 53). So, why are half of minimum wage workers older than 24? There are a lot more adults than teenagers and college-aged kids in this society. The fact that there are significantly more people in the adult category than the category of young people will distort any simple comparison between these two groups.

For a different take on why it's essential to account for population sizes when comparing groups, we'll look at a statistical comparison that affects nerds. I've heard from friends that White Americans in the United States spend more money than Asian Americans on merchandise related to Japanese Cartoons. I haven't verified this to be true. However, even though it goes against the stereotype that Asians are more likely to purchase these geeky products from the country of the rising sun, it wouldn't surprise me if the statement was correct. The reason? Over ten times more people can be identified as White than can be identified as Asian in the United States [4]. The average White American only has to be slightly more than a tenth as likely to buy this dorky paraphernalia as the average Asian American to purchase more of these items collectively. The point is, accounting for the differences in population sizes is crucial if you want to compare statistics between any two groups accurately.

Many try to refute the fact that most minimum wage workers are teenagers by arguing that "the average age of those earning the minimum wage is 35." The statistic that they cite may be real, but those who do a little digging and comprehend basic math beyond the third grade quickly realize they're being misled. What do we learn in the fourth grade that is useful to us in examining statistics? There are three easy ways to determine central tendencies of data, mean (a.k.a. average), median, and mode. Some try to confuse the public by purposefully reporting the calculation that best suits their agenda. Which central tendency calculation is most likely not very accurate when calculating the average age of minimum wage workers? The mean (aka the average). Why? The range of ages for minimum wage workers is high, so significantly older workers will skew the result. Let's demonstrate why the calculations (and their subsequent reporting use) are so misleading:

Here are ten random numbers that could represent the age of a minimum wage worker—16, 16, 17, 18, 19, 22, 35, 41, 56, 70.

Mean: To find the mean of these ages, add all of these numbers and divide them by the total amount of numbers in the data set. We get 310 when we add all the numbers together. Now, divide 310 (sum) by 10 (total amount of numbers); this leaves us with **31** as our mean. That leaves us with 6 out of 10 of the ages in our data set that are at least 9 years younger than the mean age of 31.

Mode: This is the easiest to calculate. The mode is the number that occurs most often in a list of numbers. The mode in our list is **16**.

Median: The Median is also easy to calculate. Arrange the numbers from smallest to largest, then locate the number in the middle. In this case, the median age is the average of 19 and 22 since there are even amounts of numbers in our data set. Therefore, the median age in our example is **20.5**.

As you can see, talking about the "average age" of minimum wage workers can be very misleading for those that do not have a background in statistics. To accurately interpret the typical age of minimum wage workers, we would require more advanced statistical tools like *standard deviation, statistical dispersion, or a graphical illustration of the entire data set*. For those without a background in statistics, common sense and basic observation tell us that a person is much more likely to be earning the minimum wage as a young or inexperienced worker than they are as an older worker with experience.

Topic 12: How has the minimum wage impacted you?

Job skills are the most important factor when determining what kind of wages a worker can expect to earn. The particular expertise that a worker possesses is what influences: demand for their labor and the supply of people they will be competing with for their next job. The number one reason minimum wage employees earn low wages is that they have little or no job skills. Therefore, the key to increasing the salary of low-skilled workers is to get them employed, so they can start gaining experience and skills on the job. As previously discussed, making it more expensive for employers to hire minimum wage workers decreases the amount of low-skilled workers they employ. Therefore, it delays the ability of those workers to gain the skills necessary to raise their incomes. Let me explain this argument with my work history.

I started earning the minimum wage at my first job working in a grocery store when I was 17. The minimum wage back then was set at $5.15 an hour. I went looking for a better paying position shortly after starting that job since I desperately needed the money to take the non-existent ladies in my life out for fun dates. The skills I picked up at the grocery store were listed on all the applications I submitted. These skills included: using a Point-of-Service gun for tracking inventory; unloading delivery trucks; using a pallet jack to move boxes around the store; cash handling skills from running the register; customer service skills from interacting with customers; and also demonstrating that I could consistently show up to work on time. This experience led me to a warehouse job, where I earned $9.50 an hour. There wasn't a chance that the warehouse would have hired me without the experience and skills I brought from my short time at the grocery store.

At my new warehouse job, I gained experience operating an electric forklift, picking and moving packages down a delivery line, and how to operate industrial machinery appropriately. A few months passed at the warehouse, and there were no signs of any pay raises coming my way. So again, I searched for different opportunities. Due to the skills I had picked up at the grocery store and warehouse, I was able to land a factory job that paid $15 an hour. By the time I reached the tender age of 22, I was offered an entry-level supervisor position at a factory for $20 an hour. You can see through my work history how I evolved from a worker with no qualifications to become a skilled blue-collar worker in just a few short years— all while attending college full-time to learn the dismal science. Most working Americans have similar stories about how they acquired skills on the job to earn higher pay.

The most challenging job for me to land was the minimum wage position. It took three years to find anybody willing to hire me. Very few employers were willing to take the risk of losing time and money, training a kid with zero work history. I often tell my friends and family that it's much easier for me to get a six-figure job now as a highly-skilled worker than it was for me to get my minimum wage job. Why? Because employers highly covet the analytical skills and experience I have and believe it is worth a high price tag. In contrast, nobody was willing to pay $5.15 an hour to babysit a short & skinny kid that didn't even know how to use a mop wringer.

In my teenage years, my friends and I would spend about two weeks each year submitting job applications. After receiving no job offers, we would become discouraged and quit filling out applications. If the minimum wage law weren't in place, we would have been able to negotiate with a business to land a job. I could plead with the hiring managers, "Hey, I'll work free for a week so you can test me out and see if I'm the kind of employee you want to hire." Not many employers would turn down an offer like that. I have absolutely no doubt that a company would have offered me a paid position once they saw that I was eager to learn and would show up on time for my shifts. For the employers who didn't hire me after the free week trial, I would still walk away with work experience to secure a paying job with a different company. Due to the minimum wage laws— Instead of being a working teenager developing skills on the job, I was an unemployed kid with a lot of free time on my hands. What did I do with that free time? I drank cheap beer with my friends (Colt 45 & Old E.), loitered at businesses, engaged in dangerous drag races with my parent's car, and performed "questionable activities" to earn spending money. What's that saying about idle hands?

I've got to ask the minimum wage supporters this question: Which of the below two scenarios is preferable?"

A world with an enforced minimum wage? Wherein I was unable to find a job because employers thought, "This pimply kid with zero work experience is simply not worth hiring at $5.15 an hour." This situation delayed my entry into the workforce until I was 17— and I only landed a position after completing countless job applications. The fact that I wasn't employed at an earlier age also enabled a dangerous teenage drinking habit because I had nothing productive to do with all my free time.

A world without a minimum wage – In this situation, I could negotiate my pay with employers and accept compensation that was below the minimum wage. This would have allowed me to land a job within my first few attempts. In that scenario: I would have begun acquiring skills at the age of 14, instead of 17; I would have had more opportunities to explore various jobs and industries while I was still young, with limited responsibilities; and I probably wouldn't have been so reckless with alcohol, since the job would have occupied a good deal of my time and required me to be sober.

Examining those two scenarios, it's no contest what would have been the better situation. I feel robbed of the many different opportunities that would have opened up to me if I had been able to negotiate my wages with employers so that I could have started working at an earlier age.

One of the more common responses I run across from supporters of the minimum wage, who have argued with me about the morality of the policy is, "People are not born equal. Therefore, we need laws like the minimum wage to help the poor get ahead." This response is a clear indication that the person I'm debating with has completely ignored everything I've said and has just been waiting to respond with one of their talking points. People with disadvantaged backgrounds are the ones getting priced out of the labor force and losing opportunities to develop skills on the job because of the price floor on wages. Having the options available to develop in-demand skills as soon as a person is eligible and willing to work will always put those who are struggling in the best position to achieve higher-paying jobs in the future.

Advocates of the minimum wage are so vehemently focused on the specific hourly pay rate of low-skilled workers that they dismiss the consequence of reduced employment from higher minimum wages. And they ignore the other significant benefits associated with having an entry-level job– chiefly, the accumulation of valuable skills that raises future incomes. Am I saying that every unskilled worker experiences the same difficulty finding a job as my friends and I did? Absolutely not. I am saying that the minimum wage reduces the labor employers purchase from unskilled employees, and therefore introduces a barrier to entry in the bottom rungs of the labor force. Some people can overcome this hurdle without any difficulty. Others are not as fortunate.

Chapter 2—Welfare

Topic 13: Good gracious, you can't seriously be against welfare programs, can you?

For countless generations, people worldwide have asked their leaders to create programs to assist struggling members of their communities. These programs have been run by charities, religious organizations, and governments, etc. With the exception of government-provided aid (*welfare*), collecting the resources to fund these programs has been mostly voluntary. Since it is necessary to impose mandatory taxes on working citizens to pay for government assistance, it should come as no surprise that there is much more controversy surrounding government aid than the support that is provided by charities and religious organizations. The social strife the government programs cause is astronomical. Taxpayers are outraged that they have to work hard day in and day out, only to have a portion of their income forcibly redirected to people who are not working. Meanwhile, the poor and advocacy groups for the poor are disgusted that taxpayers seem unsympathetic with the tragic plight experienced by the less fortunate. These grievances from both sides of the argument usually crowd out the question that most people fail to ask—Does welfare help or hurt the poor?

Just so we're all on the same page: I am defining welfare as financial and material aid that the government offers to the; poor, elderly, and disabled in our society. Government aid usually comes in the form of direct monetary payments to the poor (welfare payments), credit for food (food stamps), housing (Section 8 & public housing), and healthcare subsidies (Medicaid), etc. My focus will be on the impact these programs have on healthy working-age citizens.

In regards to the healthy beneficiaries of welfare, the stated intention of these programs is excellent— "Help those in dire financial situations lift themselves out of poverty." I'm entirely in support of that. I honestly couldn't imagine a person who would be against the noble goal of helping people get on their feet. Unfortunately, when we take a good hard look at the outcomes of people who receive government welfare, it becomes clear that these programs have a very long track record of keeping these recipients in a constant state of poverty. The main problem introduced by welfare programs, is that healthy citizens usually are only allowed to receive government aid after being *means-tested*. Means testing refers to the process of government administrators checking the applicants' income and assets to make sure that their income and assets are low enough to qualify for the programs they are applying for. This requirement creates a powerful incentive for healthy citizens with no/low skills to reduce/eliminate their wages and traceable resources to qualify for these programs.

Making the logical claim that "Welfare is great at providing short-term relief to the poor, but often comes at the cost of imposing negative long-term consequences such as dependence and sustained poverty for the recipients" is a losing argument. The problem economists run into when talking about welfare programs' adverse side effects is that the arguments against welfare programs are technical/long-winded, and therefore not intuitive. In contrast, the statements made by supporters of government welfare programs are filled with short slogans that appeal instantly to universally shared experiences/emotions regarding economic struggle.

Topic 14: How does welfare hurt the poor?

Welfare hurts the poor by disincentivizing the people who receive government aid from moving up the career ladder and discouraging them from acquiring capital to invest in their own futures. To introduce these two inflammatory points, I will do a very "scientific analysis" by using anecdotal stories from the welfare recipients that I know.

I have a friend named John Doe, who is living off of the aid he receives from welfare. I'll be using John's experience with government programs to illustrate how welfare disincentivizes people from moving up the career ladder. Just to give you a little bit of background information on John, he is in his late twenties with a live-in girlfriend and an adorable 3-year-old child. John has always been very candid with people about the benefits he and his girlfriend receives from the government, so I have no problem sharing their situation:

1. Section 8 Housing—John and his family live in an

81

apartment, where they pay $200 a month in rent. These apartments typically rent for about $850 a month. When you do the math, that means a Section 8 voucher is covering $ 650 of John's rent.

2. Food stamps—John and his family receive food stamps totaling around $320 a month.

3. Welfare payments—In the past, John has received an assistance check for $840 a month.

If we total it up, John is pulling in around $1,810 a month in benefits from various welfare programs. For the sake of simplicity, there are additional programs that John draws aid from that I did not mention like Medicaid, and programs with small monthly payouts.

To better understand why John has decided to live off welfare instead of working to earn a paycheck, I'll explain how getting a job would affect John's income. If John was offered a full-time job that pays $10.10 an hour (the supposed living wage), would he be better off in the short-term taking that job? No. If John were to take the job, he would lose some or all of the benefits he and his girlfriend are receiving from the government, which at present is worth more than the $10.10 an hour he would be offered to take the job. You can do the math for yourself, and you'll see that the welfare package that John and his family are currently receiving is more valuable than the monthly wage of around $1,755.38 (pre-tax) he would be earning from a job that pays $10.10 an hour:

(Hourly Wage * Average Weekly Work Hours * Average Weeks in a Month) = (10.10 * 40 * 4.345 = 1,755.38).

Given a choice between these two options— John is probably going to make the rational economic decision and postpone taking the job because, in the short-run, he receives more benefits by not working.

I don't judge John's character at all. He is an excellent father to his kid. To tell you the truth, if I were in his exact situation, I would probably choose to stay on welfare as well. Some would say that John is gaming the system. The reality is that John is just reacting logically to the bad incentive that is being offered to him. It would be ridiculously difficult in the short-term to walk away from the guaranteed sources of government income. Especially when the alternative for John is to take on the risk of getting a job at a lower or equal benefit that requires him to work, and that may or may not lead to stable employment.

If John stays on welfare, his income will always be capped at what he can receive in government benefits. Meanwhile, John's friends (including myself) who are still in the workforce will be continually gaining more and more skills at their jobs. John will be left with the same skills/income potential he had when he first started receiving welfare, while John's friends will accumulate pay raises to go along with their on the job skills development. As long as John qualifies for such a generous welfare package, he will probably continue to stay out of the labor force. In the long run, this scenario will keep John from finding decent-paying work, as his skills are not being developed while he is unemployed and on welfare. This stagnation in John's skills will make it difficult, if not impossible, for him to find a job that offers him a high enough benefit to abandon his welfare package, resulting in John staying on government assistance for as long as he is eligible.

It's not just the poor who can find themselves trapped in situations of skills stagnation due to another party incentivizing them to stay unemployed. This scenario also happens to wealthy homemakers who get married at a very young age and are lured out of the labor force by their spouses. It is not uncommon to see affluent couples come to arrangements where one partner stays at home with the kids and tends to the household's affairs while their partners go to work. If these stay at home parents were ever to divorce their working partners, they would find themselves at risk for a financial catastrophe. The years they spent at home all but guarantees that they will not have the job skills to find employment that will support their lifestyles after a divorce. That is why the non-working spouses are inclined to fight tooth and nail for large divorce settlements.

Let's move on to my second point about how welfare keeps the poor in a constant state of poverty: *Welfare discourages people from saving money to invest in themselves.* The government doesn't want the wealthy or upper-middle-class to receive welfare, which is why a welfare applicant/recipient has to regularly report both their income and assets to the government to qualify for government assistance. The result is that most welfare recipients will be incentivized to spend their money as quickly as they receive it. Why? Any assets that the applicants own will count against them when determining the government benefits they are eligible to receive. Under the *means-tested* welfare system, people on assistance will find it difficult to accumulate assets to improve their employment prospects without losing some or all of their government benefits. This situation makes it much more difficult for a person on government assistance to save money to: pay for training programs to get the skills necessary to land a better job; cover the costs of moving to areas with a larger number of better-paying jobs; and to buy a car to drive to job interviews, etc.

Since welfare recipients with bank accounts are required to send their bank statements in with their application for government aid, they are incentivized to hide the money that they don't spend in the form of untraceable cash. The disadvantages of cash are: it loses value due to inflation, and people holding large sums of paper money are vulnerable to getting robbed in their homes or on the streets. In the past, I learned that many of the people at the food pantry I used to volunteer at hoarded cash instead of depositing savings in the bank. Some of these people would ask me if they could give me money to make an online

purchase for them with my credit card. The reason why they did

this is simple—they couldn't put a lot of money in the bank

where the government could see it while they were receiving

welfare benefits, and online purchases often require a debit or

credit card.

Topic 15: Why do economists say that welfare keeps the poor dependent?

The two main reasons that welfare policies keep the recipient's dependent on government aid are:

1. Welfare incentivizes failure and punishes success for unskilled workers—The less money you earn from working, the more benefits you get out of welfare. The reverse of that is, the more money you make at work, the fewer benefits you receive from welfare programs. As a result, people with no/low skills will act rationally in the short-term to maximize their current welfare benefits by remaining unemployed or working fewer hours to reduce their income. These benefits come at the expense of developing skills at a job and therefore stunt the recipients' earning potential.

2. Means-tested programs prevent capital accumulation—

Means-tested programs require welfare applicants to have low income & limited resources to qualify for the aid. Therefore, *means-testing forces the poor to stay impoverished to continue receiving government benefits.* If a person has savings in the bank allocated for education, transportation, or equipment that can help improve their ability to find a job, it will reduce or eliminate the benefits they are eligible to receive from welfare programs. Welfare proponents seek to counter the harmful effects of means-testing by proposing the government remove means-testing when determining whether a person qualifies for government benefits. The problem with that solution is, there is a fiscal stability issue when the entire country is eligible to apply for government benefits!

Low-income workers who forego work to collect welfare aren't lazier than middle-income earners or high-income earners per se; they are just the only group of workers who could quit their jobs and receive similar incomes from welfare benefits. Most economists would expect middle-income and high-income earners to drop out of the labor force if the government were to continue increasing welfare benefits to match the compensation of the highest income earners in this country. The only people that would continue showing up at their jobs would be workers that occupy professions that provide non-monetary compensation (e.g., Actors, Artists, and Singers that receive fame and adulation for their work).

Despite the best intentions, government assistance programs make it so that poor people have a more challenging time acquiring skills and discourage them from saving money to invest in themselves. That's why many economists say that welfare programs keep people poor and subsidizes failure. A person receiving welfare is incentivized to trade the useful long-term skills that could be gained on the job for meager short-term payments that keep them in a prolonged state of poverty. It would be irrational for them to work, as long as the government's welfare benefits are close to the pay they can receive with their skill level. For analogy purposes— How many people would you expect to see working hard, and sweating it out at the gym, if the Fitness Fairy appeared to everyone on the planet and made the following declaration: "Hey Bros and Lady-Bros, I'm going to change how your body works. From here on out, everyone that chooses not to exercise will receive a regular supply of bro-dust that will instantly give the user an ok beach body (no rolls but no abs). For those of you who do attempt to exercise, you're on your own."?

Topic 16: Don't corporations receive more welfare from the government than poor people?

The question of who receives more money from the government, corporations or poor people depends entirely on how you ask the question. If you're asking, "Do American corporations as a *whole* receive more welfare from the American government than private citizens as a *whole*?" Then the answer is no. If you're asking, "Do *individual* corporations receive more money in subsidies than *individual* welfare recipients?" Then the answer is yes. Corporations as a whole received about $100 billion in 2014 from the federal government [5], while the Medicaid program alone cost the government around $476 billion in the same year [6]. Why do corporations individually receive more money than individual Americans? The scale of the expenses is entirely different between these two groups. A single corporation requires a lot more money to run their day to day operations than an individual household.

In any case, I see a lot of angry people who bring up the fact that corporations receive welfare. I'm with them in the need for the government to get rid of corporate subsidies. Those subsidies cause a lot of manipulation in the market: the business that receives government assistance will have an unfair competitive advantage over the companies that don't; unproductive companies are propped up with government money; and organizations are inclined to bribe politicians to support these subsidies. I don't like that welfare proponents' who are upset about corporate subsidies turn around and use their anger to justify government programs for needy people—two wrongs don't make a right. Corporate subsidies create destructive behaviors from businesses that reduce overall production, and welfare creates disincentives for people to work and develop their skills.

Topic 17: Is there any form of aid that works?

In my opinion, private charity tends to be the best method to combat poverty. Charitable organizations can provide poor people with access to food, shelter, healthcare (via free clinics), etc. People are confused when I tell them that I support private charity but condemn government assistance. "How is a person that gets food from a soup kitchen any better off in the long run than a person that collects food stamps?" is the standard response I hear. The difference between charity and welfare is that charity does not discourage people from working and gaining skills, unlike welfare. The two main reasons charity does not disincentivize people from working are: charity, unlike welfare, isn't ordinarily means-tested, and living off of charity can be a very unpleasant experience.

The ability to acquire aid without being subjected to means-testing allows charity recipients to keep a job while still getting the material support they need to survive. In comparison, government aid receivers are likely to lose some or all of their benefits if they collect income or acquire assets. The reason why charity doesn't have to means-test the people they serve is that unlike with welfare, people will wean themselves off of charity as they gain income. Understanding why this is the case will require us to explore how people receive aid from the government versus how people receive charitable assistance.

Food from the Government—A person can apply for government food stamps with an application that can be submitted online. If the applicant meets all the qualifications, they'll receive a monthly stipend for food on a plastic card (SNAP benefits, a.k.a. Food Stamps). This form of payment will be accepted at most local grocery stores.

Food from a Charity—To obtain food from a private charity, a person has to show up every day at their local soup kitchens during specified times. These meals are often served in a cafeteria setting. An alternative to the soup kitchens is food banks. Food banks allow an individual to collect food from a general pantry at specified times during the week.

Shelter from the Government—A person can apply for a Section 8 housing voucher at a Housing and Urban Development Office (HUD). If they qualify for this program, the government will give them a monthly voucher for their rent. The government will then pay their landlord the voucher amount, and the individual is responsible for any remaining balances. There are also public housing properties run by the government, where the rent is heavily subsidized.

Shelter from a Charity—There is no means testing required to receive shelter from most charities. A person just has to show up at specified times at a center that houses the homeless. They will most likely be sharing the facility they stay at with a large number of other people. In the morning, the shelter operators usually force the inhabitants out to engage with society (also, the facility needs the space for other public services). Charities also offer alternative long-term housing solutions as well. One of these alternatives is to live in a halfway home with some potentially unsavory characters.

Cash from the Government—A person can apply for either unemployment benefits or the Temporary Assistance for Needy Families Program (TANF). If they qualify, they will periodically receive a check or direct deposit from the government.

Cash from a Charity—Charities typically don't offer their recipient's regular cash disbursements. Most charities limit providing cash to the needy, as the charities cannot track what items recipients choose to spend that money on.

Healthcare from the Government—An individual can get Medicaid by applying online via the Healthcare.Gov website or visiting their local public services office. Once they are approved, they will receive an insurance card that is accepted by a large number of healthcare providers. The recipients may be subject to some cost-sharing, depending on their level of financial need.

Healthcare from a Charity—To obtain healthcare from private charities, a poor person will usually have to apply at a free clinic through an application that's somewhat similar to the Medicaid application. The clinic will then allow the applicant to schedule appointments or walk-ins for preventative and urgent care. The downside of private charity is the wait time is often very long, and the face-to-face time a person receives with a physician is usually brief.

Can you see the difference between receiving assistance from the government and receiving aid from private charities? Getting help from a charity is much less desirable when compared to the government option. When dealing with private charity: a person has limited benefit options, has to associate with "interesting" strangers, and often has to travel to where the assistance is being offered to receive the aid. On the other hand, the person receiving government aid gets vouchers from the government to use at their discretion. Welfare recipients can choose: where they want to live with Section 8 Vouchers, which grocery stores they want to shop at with Food Stamps, and can schedule appointments with most doctors and clinics with Medicaid.

Due to shortsighted logic, most people would say that welfare is better than charity, as it makes life substantially easier for the recipients. Government aid is simpler to obtain, provides more flexible benefit options, and is much more generous than private charity. The pitfall of government welfare is that due to the generosity and means-testing of these programs, it disincentivizes many able-bodied people from being employed. Welfare recipients are offered some financial security if they don't work, but they can lose that security if they get a job. In comparison, the unsavory nature of receiving charitable benefits serves as a strong incentive for people to get out of poverty so that they never again have to stand in a charity line to get their dinner.

For the same reason, a doctor doesn't want their patients to live sedentary lifestyles; an economist doesn't want people to be out of work for long periods. Both scenarios lead to decay. A sedentary lifestyle rots your body. Being unemployed rots your skills and diminishes your future earning potential. Therefore, any program designed to provide aid to the poor must be extremely careful not to discourage the recipients from working. Welfare is excellent at providing short term relief but comes at the cost of enticing people to forego employment to continue collecting benefits. Regarding charity, you can step into a homeless shelter and experience for yourself firsthand why very

few people in this country would want to make a lifestyle out of

receiving charity.

Topic 18: *Without a minimum wage, welfare, and all the other government protections, Americans would be as poor as people living in developing countries.*

Americans aren't rich because we have laws that set minimum wages and provide welfare programs to the less fortunate. Those policies were put in place on a federal level after the United States established itself as one of the world's wealthiest countries. If making the citizens in a country rich just required lawmakers to craft rules controlling the wages employers have to pay their employees, and create welfare programs to redistribute wealth to the poor— then every country in the world would have well-off citizens. Many poor countries have tried both of those strategies at one point or another in their history. These policies end with the same results— reduced economic mobility for their low-skilled workers and welfare recipients. As we've previously discussed: minimum wage policies reduce opportunities for low-skilled workers, and welfare policies disincentivize the accumulation of skills and capital.

The short answer for why we see the wealth disparity between a rich country like the United States, and a poor country such as Vietnam, is that there is a huge productivity gap between the workforce in both countries. Americans are a lot wealthier than the Vietnamese because American workers produce more goods and services than Vietnamese workers. An average American employee creates about eight times more goods and services, as measured by value than the average Vietnamese employee [7]. Before you get the wrong idea, American workers aren't "naturally" eight times stronger, faster, or more intelligent than their Vietnamese equivalent. The average American worker might be a slightly better performer, all else equal, but it's not nearly enough to explain the productivity difference when compared to their Vietnamese counterpart.

Why is the productivity rate between these two groups of workers so different if both the groups' physical and intellectual potential is somewhat similar? It's because Americans have accumulated a lot more capital and have acquired the skills to wield these resources in their production process. In other words, Vietnamese workers don't have the equipment and machinery that make American workers so unbelievably productive, and even if that capital appeared in Vietnam overnight, they would not have the collective knowledge to operate and maintain all that equipment.

Instead of producing a few pairs of jeans per day with sewing machines as they often do in Vietnam, the American factory workers use industrial garment manufacturing machines to turn out hundreds of jeans per hour. Instead of using farm animals and outdated tools to plow a few acres of land a week, the American farmers use modern tractors that can do the same amount of work in a fraction of the time. Instead of using bikes and small trucks to deliver packages, the American delivery services use planes, trains, and trucks the size of houses to move billions of parcels every year.

The solution for how to end Vietnamese poverty is simple. The Vietnamese people need to replace the simple tools in their country with sophisticated modern machines to boost the number of goods and services they can produce and distribute. As the amount of capital in their country increases, their workforce will gradually develop the skills to use and manage these resources to create more stuff and raise their living standards. There are two ways for them to accumulate capital, and they are as follows:

1. The first way for an economy to build up capital is to divert some resources away from consumer goods (food, clothing, shelter, etc.) to purchase capital goods (factory machines, tractors, trucks, among others) from developed countries. Reducing consumer goods in an economy is not a very popular move in a country where people live hand to mouth.

2. The second way to increase capital would be to have foreigners invest in building factories in developing

countries. These factories typically start out producing easily manufactured goods such as clothing and gradually start to churn out goods that require more advanced capital to manufacture, such as electronics and cars. Why would foreigners invest in developing economies? Labor in developing countries is initially very cheap when compared to labor in developed countries. The labor savings allow companies to offset their capital costs and the price of shipping the finished goods to their home countries. Unfortunately, foreign investment is also not a very popular solution, as the wages the factory workers earn in developing countries are often labeled as being "exploitive." This criticism goes against the fact that the salaries at foreign-owned factories are often higher than what the locals can earn anywhere else in their country.

The only way for a country to develop is to increase its workers' access to machinery and equipment to increase production. Fortunately, despite the unpopularity of the two capital accumulation methods I noted above, Vietnam has been embracing both of these approaches. As a result, Vietnamese households' average income has been growing year after year, as capital and skills are being developed in their country. Will their quality of life catch up with that of Americans soon? Probably not. Going from a poor developing country to an industrial superpower is not an overnight process.

Chapter 3—Profit & Wealth

Topic 19: The enormous profits earned by corporations in this country is definitive proof that Americans are being robbed blind!

I have never fully understood the blind outrage that people have with companies earning profits. The belief is, "If a company or person makes a lot of money, they must be doing it at other people's expense." Of course, I'm aware that there are always a few corporations that engage in some unlawful activities to spike their earnings. However, evidence of their wrongdoings normally surfaces and results in legal penalties and market consequences (e.g., losing customers). The vast majority of companies earn their money legitimately by producing goods and services to trade with consumers. The customers of most businesses are perfectly willing to pay for the products that these companies have for sale. Companies that earn an obscene amount of money do so because of the massive demand that they encounter for their products, coupled with their ability to supply them at a better price and quality than their competitors. To understand how businesses are legitimately earning their money, let's dive into the operating model of a large corporation that is routinely scrutinized for their enormous profits.

ExxonMobil is a company that has consistently been one of the most profitable companies in America [8]. Exxon earns most of its money by pumping oil from the ground and refining oil into gasoline, petrochemicals, and other miscellaneous petroleum products. It should be pretty clear why Exxon earns a ton of money. They successfully compete in the energy industry by *supplying* the best products at the best prices; and people all around the world are continually *demanding* more of Exxon's products to support their day-to-day lifestyles (I'm not going to get into a debate about global warming in this book). Exxon's industry is not an easy business to operate in. Their primary commodity, "oil," is tough and costly to extract from the ground and refine into the products consumers use (gasoline, heating oil, jet fuel, etc.). If you look at how Exxon operates on a day to day basis, you'll quickly realize that this corporation is earning their money the hard way.

1. To produce any of their refined oil products, Exxon has to first hire teams of geologists to hunt for areas with oil resources.

2. After a potential oil field is located, Exxon has to pay a team of lawyers/scientists/engineers to acquire the rights to drill on the land, study the environmental impact, assess risk, and compile safety proposals to protect themselves from litigation.

3. Once all that is done, Exxon has to set up a local infrastructure around the field to support its operations. The infrastructure might include roads to help transport supplies and electricity generation stations to power all the heavy equipment they'll be using.

4. Exxon can then bring in the equipment to drill their first

holes. This machinery can cost millions of dollars, with an additional cost of tens of thousands of dollars for transport to their respective fields. A crew of drillers will use this equipment to drill test holes to see if there is any oil at the site. Some of these areas will turn out to have little or no oil at all. If this is the case, the oil company can lose millions of dollars.

5. If the field possesses a significant amount of recoverable oil, the company will build more permanent infrastructure at the site. This infrastructure will help supply the operation with the equipment necessary to extract the oil from the ground. Also, pipelines and additional roads might have to be created off-site to carry the oil out of the field.

6. Large teams of drillers and support staff will then pump the oil out of the ground and prepare it for transportation or temporary storage.

7. The extracted oil is then shipped out in huge tankers, pipelines, trains, or trucks to an oil refinery that can be hundreds if not thousands of miles away.

8. Once the oil arrives at the refinery, it is placed in large machines that heat it to vaporize and separate the oil into many different petroleum distillates. This process is called fractional distillation.

9. The separated liquids are then transported to processing plants to get them ready to be turned into final products such as gasoline, heating oil, cooking fuels, waxes, among others.

10. The finished goods are then transferred out to be sold at wholesale and retail locations around the world.

All the work Exxon puts into making sure there is: gas for you to drive your car, gas to heat your home, and gas to cook your food, etc., is why they earn a ton of money. There is a high demand for their products, and they go to extraordinary lengths to make sure they can supply it to their consumers. If people understood the difficult steps it takes for businesses in every industry to produce the goods and services they consume daily, they would realize why there is nothing wrong with a company earning considerable profits for the most part.

If corporations weren't receiving a profit for all the hard work they put into their operations, they would have no ability/incentive to operate. Everyone would be much poorer without the plethora of products and services they produce. Furthermore, when we go back and look at how much total product Exxon creates and how much money they keep as profit, it becomes clear that Exxon doesn't have a large net income. I won't keep you in suspense: at the end of the day, Exxon holds on to less than ten cents of every dollar that they collect from their customers after paying for expenses and taxes [8]! Why does Exxon's total annual profit amount to tens of billions of dollars in most years? The sheer quantity of goods they supply to their

customers is astronomical, and the products they sell have

traditionally been in extremely high demand.

Topic 20: How does the economy benefit from people earning profits?

Critics of the free market are strongly vocal about the fact that the pursuit of profits can lead people to lie, cheat, and steal. My response to that is, the same statement can be made about alternative economic systems (government-controlled). I would argue that the alternative systems make it far easier for corruption to occur in the production process since government officials can and will abuse their political power to enrich themselves. Using the power of their office, politicians can use tax dollars to prop up unproductive companies and legal action to crush competitors that could offer a better service at a better price than their cronies (a topic for another book). As I stated before, most people in a free market who are consistently earning profits are doing it by serving their customers well. Their ability to deliver for the consumer is evident from the fact that their customers keep returning to purchase their products. In this section, I want to discuss a few different ways that profit is essential for maintaining a productive and growing economy.

Profit drives people to move heaven and earth to produce goods and services for people they usually don't even know. Profit allows people to help others (we work hard to create goods and services for others to consume) while assisting themselves (we get paid back with the goods and services that other people produce). The beauty of this is that a producer doesn't have to care about the people they serve. The only thing suppliers have to care about is making money for themselves and their families. Businesses are continually producing more goods and services for consumers to consume to earn money for themselves. The same is true for the average worker. Workers are pursuing profit for themselves and their families in the form of their paychecks. The majority of us don't go to work because we care about our fellow man. We go to work so that we can get paid. Take the paycheck away, and the vast majority of people will stop showing up at their jobs.

Profit is one of the most accurate indicators of which products and services that people want to consume. Suppliers know to produce more of the goods that are flying off the shelves and generating enormous profits, and less of the items that are just sitting in stores collecting dust. Businesses will be rewarded with higher earnings if they produce more of the things consumers are vigorously demanding at prices consumers are willing to pay. They'll be punished with bankruptcy if they choose to make overpriced and inferior products (the car manufacturers in Detroit, the camera makers at Kodak, and the executives at Circuit City can attest to this). Why is it a good thing that some businesses go bankrupt? Because poorly run companies are wasting resources producing items that people are not utilizing.

Lastly, the pursuit of wealth and profit encourages people to delay their consumption today so that they can invest in projects that will increase future production. Instead of spending every cent of my paycheck when I was young on

118

whiskey and chasing women, I invested a portion of it to reap the future returns. The money that I didn't spend on personal consumption was being redirected by my bank and financial advisor to people who were forced to create future value if they wanted to pay back their loan or grow their company's market value. This investment resulted in the creation of more goods and services for consumers.

With regards to the rich, when you dig into the personal finances of high net worth individuals, you begin to see that the majority of the income they earn is not spent on private consumption. It's extremely rare to see high net worth individuals with non-investment expenses and assets that equal up to even half their net worth. Their money is mostly used to help advance the plight of the lower/middle class via investments. Now, does that mean the rich care about the little guys? Probably not any more or less than any of the rest of us care about strangers. The wealthy care about growing and maintaining their wealth just like most of us middle-class folks. The only way for them to do that is to engage in or associate themselves with activities that create

value for the economy (the production of goods and services for

consumers).

Topic 21: Since the wealthy own most of the capital, isn't it impossible for ordinary citizens to gain wealth?

Many Americans are living paycheck to paycheck in today's economy. There is a pervasive belief among the younger generation that the large wealth concentration among the wealthy is the cause for this situation. "The rich are taking all the wealth for themselves and leaving nothing for the rest of us!" is the sentiment that I hear a lot from my generation. The result of the supposed wealth hoarding among the rich is that the indigent and middle class have no chance of gaining the resources needed to move up the economic ladder, thus repeating the cycle of money accumulating in the hands of the few. I want to examine the premise behind this argument. Do wealthy people really hoard resources, and does the economy only benefit people who are already affluent?

To start, let's ask some quick questions about what rich people do with their money:

1. Do the wealthy loan any of their assets out via bank deposits or investments?

2. Do wealthy people hire any workers to operate their businesses?

3. Do the wealthy purchase any goods and services from other people?

If the rich engage in any of the activities mentioned above, their assets have to flow to people who can make good use of these resources. In other words, the money from well off citizens will be borrowed and spent by anybody involved in producing products for consumers. Let me explain the results of these actions individually:

1. **What happens if the rich loan their money out via bank deposits or investments?**— When a wealthy person deposits their funds in a bank or invests it directly

into the financial markets, the money gets funneled to somebody who needs it and can be productive with the money. If the cash is deposited in a bank, it gets lent out to borrowers who apply for and are approved for a loan. If the funds are invested in the financial markets, they can be used to buy partial ownership in a company (stocks) or used to purchase corporate debt (bonds). The people who are borrowing the money through loans or bonds or selling shares in their company can use the funds coming from the rich to build a new business or expand an existing one. The result is more jobs for workers and the production of more goods and services for consumers.

People who take out personal loans to purchase consumer goods to improve their quality of life (e.g., cars, houses, to name a few) are forced to create value. Lending out money for personal consumption leads to productive economic activities because it often requires the borrowers to work to produce goods and services to pay back the loans, whereas just giving people free money requires no further action on the part of the recipient. In a "free market," banks will make lending decisions based on risk. They will grant loans to borrowers who are likely to produce goods and services to generate the income necessary to repay the bank and deny loans to people who aren't expected to be productive enough to pay them back.

In any case, the money from the rich is not left idle in some vault. Money that does not get put to use is quickly eroded away by *inflation*. Cash is like most commodities out there; you either use it or watch time eat away at its value. The rich "lend out" their excess funds to productive people to maintain and grow their wealth. This process is a win-win for everybody involved.

2. What happens if the affluent hire workers to work in their businesses?— Regardless of how low the starting wages of any position is, workers gain money and skills by being employed. These skills allow them to demand higher salaries. If a worker is frugal with their paychecks, they will reach a point where they can use their savings to acquire capital to start a business or pay for education to improve their skills further.

3. What happens if the rich purchase goods and services from businesses that they don't own?— If the rich purchase products, somebody has to produce it. Therefore, the wealthy will have to trade some of their assets to people willing to provide the goods and services they want to buy. The people in the organizations that are supplying those items will be able to use the proceeds from these sales to build up their wealth.

I can provide numerous examples from my family history on how my Grandparents, Parents, and Aunts/Uncles were able to improve their standard of living by engaging in the activities mentioned above with people who were much wealthier than themselves. My family came to the U.S. after leaving a country that went into the hands of brutal communists. When they got to this country: they didn't speak English, they had job skills that didn't transfer well to the career opportunities available in this country, the culture was radically different from what they were used to, and like most new immigrants to this country, they were stigmatized for being foreigners. They were about as poor as anybody can get in the United States. As is the case with many Asian immigrants in America during that time, the first jobs they were able to land was work that paid below the minimum wage (under the table). At those jobs: they learned English by interacting with coworkers and customers, they learned how small businesses operated in this country, and they were able to network with other people to find opportunities to increase their skills. My family used the skills they gained at their initial jobs to get higher-paying positions and eventually were able to save enough money to open their own businesses. The whole transition from poor refugees to middle-class citizens took very little time for them. My grandparents retired comfortably, and most of my family now earn what can be considered upper-middle-class incomes. To recapitulate, my once dirt-poor family took advantage of the fact that: *wealthy people hire others* and that *the wealthy purchase goods and services* from other people, to build wealth and create opportunities for themselves and their children. How would my family's journey from piss-poor refugees to affluent first-world citizens be possible if the wealth hoarding of wealthy Americans suppressed economic mobility?

A person that believes in entrenched wealth can counter my example with the statement, "Your family's experience is the exception and not the rule. A lot of immigrants that come to the United States stay poor." I would respond to that statement by showing them statistics that illustrate that a large number of

Asian American families that came from third world countries, usually as destitute refugees, out-earn a large number of Americans born into middle-class and wealthy families. Asian American immigrants can do this by outworking the *average* native-born American and pursuing skills or producing products that employers and customers are demanding (instead of blindly pursuing passions that may or may not work out). We see this same scenario being played out in a lot of immigrant groups from different nationalities. As long as "hard work," long-term planning, and delayed gratification is embedded in their culture, members of poor immigrant groups can come to America with nothing and end up in affluence. When we look at the incomes of Americans of East Asian, Indian, or Nigerian descent, it is evident that they have higher salaries than average native-born Americans, which had more wealth available to them growing up [9]. America has large numbers of successful: East Asian small business owners, Indian doctors, Nigerian businessmen, and East Asian computer programmers, among others (how's that for stereotyping?). These immigrants have lived through poverty that most native-born Americans couldn't imagine, yet it is not unusual for them to come to this free country and earn incomes in the six-figure range within their lifetimes.

Switching gears: on the macro level, the fact that wealth can't be hoarded is also the reason why impoverished countries have been able to increase their national incomes in recent years. If income were completely limited to past wealth accumulation, countries like China and India would not be posting such staggering annual gains in GDP. The relatively recent change from command economies to slightly more free-market-oriented economies has led to a boom in production in these countries. One of the most important ways these developing countries have been able to gain wealth is by attracting international investment from developed countries like the United States (e.g., taking advantage of the assets from the rich that we talked about earlier). The wealth that is supposedly hoarded by the affluent in developed countries has been invested in factories and jobs in poor countries. The exposure to foreign capital during the production cycle in these developing countries increases the quantity and quality of skills among their workers. The result of all this foreign investment is that the quality of life in developing countries increases exponentially year after year. All of that development is made possible from the assets that supposedly only benefits the already wealthy.

The flaws arising from the view that wealth can be hoarded in a free market leaves out facts like:

1. The wealthy have to trade their accumulated assets to acquire goods and services from other people.

2. The people who own the capital aren't the only ones benefitting from that capital. For example, the company owners own all the machinery in a factory. However, the workers utilize that machinery to gain skills on the job to

increase their productivity. Productivity gains from the use of capital results in a worker's ability to get better pay in the future (if they keep their skills relevant) and lowers the prices of goods and services for all consumers.

3. To accumulate all of the wealth in the world, a person would have to do one of two things:

Produce a product that loses all of its value once it's sold, but it is so amazing that everybody on the planet was willing to trade all of their money, houses, cars, and any other material belongings they own to obtain this magical item. This outcome would also require that one single person produce, distribute, and collect the money from their customers without employing any of their own workers or utilizing the services of any other businesses. Hiring another person or company would require them to transfer wealth to their workers.

Or

They would have to steal every single bit of property in the world singlehandedly and force everybody into involuntary servitude to serve them and only them.

Why are there so many people living paycheck to paycheck in this country if the wealthy aren't hoarding away their assets? It's not a mystery when we do a thorough audit of the financial situations of these people. The behavior of most citizens is not conducive to building wealth. That is because the majority of people are spending their money as quickly as they're earning it. What's great about my generation is that we actually document our terrible money habits on social media platforms with selfies and videos showing us: going out to eat more times than we should, drinking at bars; going on vacations; and going into debt to buy things we can't afford (e.g., homes, cars, phones, technology, entertainment, and expansive wardrobes). No matter how much income you have coming in, if you spend all your money on depreciating assets, you will end up flat broke (entertainers and athletes can do a much better job explaining this than any economist).

Topic 22: Does excessive profit hurt the average citizen?

Consumers are trading their money to obtain the goods and services that businesses create and distribute. People often assume that because producers are left with enormous profits after paying off their expenses, that customers are being overcharged, and workers are being underpaid. This situation leads many to ask one of the most misunderstood questions in economics, "Does profit limit the number of goods and services available to consumers?". The answer is yes and no. Profit does limit the number of goods and services for consumption in the *short run*, but profit expands the available amount of goods and services people can consume in the *long run*. Let me explain this paradox by talking about the options producers have when profit is made:

1. Producers can consume their profit by buying stuff for personal use or paying out any surpluses to themselves and

their employees. **This type of spending increases the number of resources available for current consumption but decreases their future productivity rates.**

2. Producers can use their profit to repair and maintain their existing capital. **This type of spending decreases the number of resources available for current consumption and maintains their current level of productivity.**

3. Producers can use their profit to invest in new capital and hire new workers. **This type of spending decreases the number of resources available for current consumption but increases their future productivity leading to increased future consumption.**

The reason that profit decreases consumer purchasing power in the short-run is that producers are diverting a large

135

portion of their earnings away from direct consumption to invest in producing *capital goods* (e.g., factory machinery, construction equipment, corporate servers, facility expansion, among others). The production of more capital goods will allow workers to produce/consume more consumer goods in the future because capital makes workers more productive. Increased productivity from capital use will raise employer demand for labor. Which results in higher pay for workers. Past profits that were reinvested into the production cycle is what allows the average American citizen today to produce and consume exponentially more goods than our counterparts in the past.

To make the relationship between spending on consumption and expenditure on capital more relatable, let's talk about an Uber driver's profits. An Uber driver has the following choices with how they can spend their earnings: they can spend it on rent, food, booze, consumer technology, and vacations (consume it); they can get car washes, oil changes, and tune-up's (maintain their capital); or they can save the money to purchase a larger more luxurious car to drive for Uber's premium service, which pays higher fares to the drivers, (invest it).

Suppose the driver spends all of their earnings on personal consumption. In this situation, they'll run their car into the ground and be unable to continue making money and providing services to their customers. Cars don't last long when you don't change the oil, spark plugs, brakes, tires, and all the other moving parts in the vehicle. To maximize their long-term earnings, the driver needs to spend as little money as they can get away with on personal consumption. That way, they can use the bulk of their earnings to maintain their current vehicle and save up for a car that will allow them to earn more money driving for Uber's premium service. Higher profits in the future will enable the driver to increase the money they have to allocate to both personal spending and investment.

What would happen if every producer in an industry were to price their goods at the cost it takes to produce them (i.e., they didn't collect a dime in profit)? Production would quickly stagnate because the businesses wouldn't have the resources available to expand their operations. In a profitless economic system, where would the money come from to purchase: new equipment, property for a second store/factory, or a truck to transport their equipment/goods? Before you say "outside investment," ask yourself the question, "why would investors invest in a company that would generate them no returns?"

The proof is in the pudding. There is a reason that countries that allow profits to be collected have the highest rates of production and consumption. Consumption, in profit driven economies, leads to economic growth because the earnings from consumer purchases are recycled back into the production process to maintain and grow the capital base. In comparison, nations that completely restrict organizations and individuals from collecting profits are unable to produce enough goods and services to feed their own citizens. There is no investment in capital without profit, as there are no excess resources or incentives for businesses to spend on capital and new labor. In profitless societies where the government completely restricts profits through excessive taxation and redistribution to the citizens, the invariable result is that the resources get consumed as soon as they're produced.

The general public is wrong to think that governments need to limit profits to make goods and services cheaper. That kind of short-term thinking is linked to the idea that there is an unchanging number of goods and services in a society that will be produced and consumed in an economy. Therefore, there is a tug of war between the profits that corporations keep and the amount of stuff ordinary people can consume.

The truth is that the number of goods and services in any society is in a constant state of flux. The more resources that an economy reinvests in capital, the more products consumers will have access to consume in the future. Conversely, the less resources an economy reinvests in capital, the less goods and services consumers will consume. Redistribution policies proposed by politicians decrease future production because the profits that business owners use to reinvest in capital would

instead be redirected to citizens who would immediately consume

it.

Chapter 4: Personal Subsidies

Topic 23: What harm do you see in helping students pay for their college education?

The government subsidizes the cost of higher education by giving out grants, providing direct federal loans and interest subsidized loans to borrowers, and creating legislation to increase the willingness of lenders to loan money to students. Most of these forms of aid are presented to students when they fill out a Free Application for Student Aid (FAFSA) form. Our politicians have done a great job of ensuring that students can finance their college education in the *short run*. As we'll discuss later, that is not necessarily a beneficial thing for young people. Below is a brief overview of these different forms of aid:

Grants— The government gives money for educational related expenses to those who have financial need. A grant is not a loan and never has to be repaid.

Direct loans to borrowers—Students can borrow money directly from the United States government instead of a bank. These loans often have lower interest rates than private student loans.

Interest subsidized loans—The government will pay the interest accrued on student loans while the borrower is still attending college.

Removal of bankruptcy protection on private student loans— The government makes it extremely difficult for borrowers to get out of paying their private student loans (i.e., the loans follow the borrowers even after they declare bankruptcy). How is this policy supposed to help the borrowers? The answer: It entices lenders to issue more student loans and charge lower interest rates because they don't have to worry about their borrowers not paying them back. The difference in the risk of repayment for student loans is why it's easier to get approved for a 100K student loan than a 5K car loan. The banks can lose money on a car loan if the borrower doesn't repay them, but it's almost impossible for Sallie Mae (a government-affiliated lender) to lose money on a student loan.

To understand why government policies aimed at helping students finance higher education produces negative results, we have to introduce the concept of *moral hazard*. A moral hazard is a situation where some of the costs or consequences are removed from a particular behavior. For example, suppose I tell my friend Don that I will pay for all of his alcoholic drinks every time we go out together. In that case, I am introducing a moral hazard by taking away the immediate financial cost for him to binge drink. As a result, Don will likely consume a lot more alcohol when he goes out with me, as opposed to when he goes out by himself or with other people. Don will still experience the non-financial costs associated with binge drinking, such as hangovers, alcohol dependence, drunk dialing exes, and the myriad of long-term health problems that are linked to excessive alcohol consumption.

The problem with moral hazards is obvious; it makes people behave more irresponsibly because they face fewer short term consequences when they engage in risky behaviors, but they'll still suffer the long-term problems associated with their actions. A society with noble intentions is not immune to the consequences that arise from the moral hazard of using government mandates and taxpayer money to tackle the goal of making colleges more affordable. Under the current policies, borrowers, lenders, and politicians act very recklessly because tax dollars and government regulations create a moral hazard by removing: the short term tuition costs from the student; and the default risk from the lender.

The moral hazard facing students from government intervention is that they can get approved for student loans to study any subject, at any accredited university where they get accepted. More often than not, the fields these students choose to pursue will not come close to providing them with the incomes needed to repay their loans and support themselves. I hear many recent college graduates complain that they are struggling to pay their bills because they are unable to land a decent paying job after graduation. Almost all of them are upset that the government and banks lent them enormous amounts of money that they can't pay back with the salaries they're earning.

The moral hazard that lenders face regarding student loans is that government policies shield them from the possibility that their student loan borrowers can default on their loans. Since it is hard for lenders to lose money on the student loans they issue, they lend out money to almost every student that applies to them. Two things would happen in a world where lenders were not facing the moral hazard of guaranteed repayment on student loans. Banks wouldn't lend people tens if not hundreds of thousands of dollars to study risky majors like social work, art, liberal arts, or even to attend college as an undeclared major. The risk of losing money on these loans would be too great. The second thing that would happen is banks would actually price the risk of default into the interest rate they charge for borrowers studying at different schools and majors.

As a side note, Banks price out interest rates depending on risk— the riskier a loan is, the higher the interest rate they charge. In the case of student loans, the government equalizes the risk of every student loan the bank makes because there is almost no chance of any student being able to discharge their student loans in bankruptcy. This policy is why the interest rate to study a guaranteed moneymaker such as engineering is the same as the interest rate to study a subject with a low chance of paying off, such as philosophy. Without bankruptcy protection, the risk of a complete default for different majors is about the same for the lender. If student loans were not exempt from bankruptcy, students studying STEM subjects at schools with a reputation for producing high-wage workers would be charged much lower interest rates than students studying graphic design at Art Schools. The drastic differences in securing a student loan and the interest rates between majors would help push students away from unemployable degrees.

The moral hazard that politicians face when issuing direct student loans is that they use the taxpayer's money instead of their own when crafting generous student aid policies. These elected officials couldn't care less about which students the government lends to and what subjects those borrowers study. They will probably not be voted out of office based on past elections if they are fiscally irresponsible. On the contrary, handing out gifts to the public at the taxpayer's expense is a must for politicians who want a long career in politics.

Every year in America, many college graduates leave school with crippling debt and then head straight to low paying jobs. *The message from society is to go to school and pursue your passion: and the politicians are all too happy to create popular legislation that ensures borrowed cash will continually rain down from the heavens to allow students to study whatever subject strikes their fancy.* In a free market, no bank in this country would let students commit that kind of financial suicide. Don't get me wrong; banks do not care much about the financial situations of young students. However, bankers are aware that it would affect their own pocketbooks when these aspiring artists, philosophers, and sociologists default on their loans. In a free market for higher education, young people would have to stop and ask some fundamental questions: "Why are so many people refusing to lend me money to study art? Why are the interest rates on student loans for philosophy so much higher than the rates to study computer science? Perhaps, I should think about whether I should go to college at this point in my life? What can I study

that will allow me to pay my bills in the future?

Topic 24: What's wrong with student grants? Even if the students don't get jobs after graduation, they'll at least receive a free education.

Due to the government intervention we discussed earlier in the book, students who get accepted into a University are generally able to secure the grants and loans necessary to finance their education. In recent years, supporters of affordable higher education have advocated that politicians use taxpayer money to allow all students to attend college for free. The problem with having a 100% publicly funded higher education system is that taxpayer money would: *enable* the future poor to waste their time pursuing worthless majors; while *subsidizing* the earning potential of the future rich that make wise educational decisions. Regardless of who pays their tuition, students who study subjects relevant to employers like Science, Technology, Engineering, and Math (STEM)— will earn high incomes post-graduation. In contrast, the kids who study subjects that do not convert well to real-world jobs (art, humanities, most social sciences, etc.) will continue to struggle financially after completing their programs

150

because they will face the same problems with unemployment, underemployment, and low wage rates.

As I stated before, every program has a cost and a benefit. The benefit of free college is pretty straightforward— Students wouldn't have the problem of tuition linked debt to worry about. People generally focus on the impact to the taxpayer when discussing the negative consequences associated with completely subsidizing the higher education industry. What isn't discussed are the costs to the students. Despite not paying any tuition, students who can cover the full cost of their tuition through grants will still have to deal with the high *opportunity costs,* aka "tradeoffs" (i.e., the alternatives they have to give up), to attend schools to study useless majors. Even without the burden of tuition, these opportunity costs can and will lead many people that pursue worthless majors down the path of financial ruin.

Opportunity Costs of College

151

1. *Missed opportunities to acquire real-world skills*—If a student is studying a useless major full-time, they're probably not working at a full-time job. Therefore, they are missing out on the chance to gain valuable skills that are relevant to employers. Instead, they are spending time pursuing a non-marketable education and giving up real-world job skills that they could have earned during the time they wasted in school. Many non-STEM students often graduate school with resumes that offer nothing of value to most employers. Students that are unable/uninterested in pursuing a major with good job prospects would be better served by building their resumes and sharpening their skillsets in the job market.

2. *Lost income*—As stated before, students studying full-time are probably not working a full-time job. Even if their tuition bills are being paid for by somebody else, students still have to eat and be sheltered during their time

at school. A lot of the debt that students incur while in college is associated with tuition *and their living expenses*. A graduate who wastes four years studying a useless major like sociology would not pile on the mountain of debt for tuition if it were paid for by tax dollars. However, they most likely will still have debt piling up from four years of living expenses that will accumulate while they are in school full-time and not working/working fewer hours.

3. *Wasting the buffer of time young adults have to experiment with career options*—One of the best things about being in your late teens and early twenties is that you have a lot of time and space to try new things and screw up. People in this age group are more likely to have limited responsibilities (e.g., no kids or expensive financial obligations.). Also, there is a high likelihood that their parents can still provide them with some support

when they fail. Due to those reasons, this is the best time for many to take risks to figure out what areas of the economy they can best earn a living in. Students wasting these years with a useless field of study will lose out on time to experiment in the job market by pursuing different occupations.

If a person can study something in a field with good job prospects, such as STEM-related subjects, then the high opportunity costs associated with attending college can be easily justified. Unfortunately, the degrees many people gravitate to in the unchecked environment of easily financed higher education is closely linked to low paying jobs and poverty. It is rarely worth the outrageous tuition prices, and more importantly, the other high opportunity costs associated with pursuing degrees that do not lead to jobs. The reality of this situation leads me to believe that no matter what the politicians say and what people want to think— FREE COLLEGE WOULD BE A DISASTER! It would help the future rich by subsidizing a productive education that they otherwise would finance privately and hurt the future poor by incentivizing them to sacrifice valuable time during their formative years pursuing crack-pipe studies.

Topic 25: How will students pay for college if politicians don't provide them with financial assistance?

The astoundingly high sticker price associated with attending a university in the United States causes many Americans to question how the average person could afford higher education without financial aid from a third party. Most people conclude that politicians must intervene to help students pay for college, to make education accessible to the masses. Advocates of continuing/expanding the current government-supported higher education system rarely ever stop and ask why college tuition is priced so high and why the prices keep dramatically increasing year after year. If you compare the historical cost of higher education with services from other industries, you'll see that the price of college has climbed much faster than most consumer goods or services for sale in America [13]. I will take some time to explain how the costs associated with a college degree in this country have gotten to the point where the average American family struggles to pay for tuition out of pocket and why the government-supported financial aid is directly responsible for the rising prices.

Take a look into the financial statements from any college, and you can see on paper where these schools are spending the tuition and fees being collected from their students. If you don't have any experience with reading accounting documents, walk onto any college campus today, and you'll be able to experience where all the money is being spent. Multi-Million-dollar stadiums, swimming pools, lush student centers, and state of the art research labs that are only used by a fraction of the student population— decorate every one of these college resorts. That's not even mentioning all the endless administrators and support staff that are employed to ensure a carefree student living experience. These are just a few examples of the outrageous ways colleges are racking up expenses. This wasteful spending is being passed onto students in the form of ridiculously high tuition prices and fees.

The lavish infrastructure projects and expensive university-sponsored events taking place on my college campus seemed insane to me when I was a student. The university tackled pricy projects like remodeling our perfectly functional library, constructing a new student recreation hall, completely renovating every single building that showed any signs of age, and hiring more and more non-faculty staff members to cater to the personal lives of the student population. As a curious young economist, it was hard not to wonder why such a significant portion of my university's annual budget was directed towards seemingly wasteful ventures.

For me, the underlying question was never about where my tuition dollars were going (as stated before, a college's financial statements can answer that question). The question I had was—How was my college, and other schools across the country, able to spend money so recklessly without going out of business? Most successful business owners know that companies have to balance the benefits of offering expensive amenities to attract customers with the prices their customers are willing to pay for their products. In other words— It's a great marketing tool to have fantastic student facilities and luxurious services on display when prospective students tour college campuses; but at the end of the day, a lot of potential students will be scared off when they see the enormous bill, they'll have to pay to cover these lavish accommodations. So, why haven't we seen college enrollment numbers fall off of a cliff as the price tag for a degree continues to skyrocket?

Colleges have no difficulty charging students absurdly high prices for tuition and fees because the moral hazard introduced by government-supported financial aid has made students completely insensitive to their tuition bills. Students who receive easy and fast approvals on their student loans don't care about the prices they're paying for school since they're taking care of their bills with borrowed cash. These kids don't understand the financial burden associated with owing such insane amounts of money because they don't have to start repaying their loans until after they graduate. Unfortunately, young people often don't have any experience with debt.

With the help of government policies, society is flooding the higher education market with cash via student loans and grants. This situation enables students to pay whatever price their college will charge them for educational related expenses. It is unlikely under the current system of government-supported financing options that students will ever *dramatically* pull back on attending college despite the price hikes. As a result of all the cash flowing into student loan borrowers, colleges are increasing their prices to collect as much of that money as they can. In the eyes of these universities, there is no shortage of cash or customers for their product. Therefore, there is no incentive for colleges to slash their expenses to keep their prices low. If the situation remains unchanged: colleges will continue to accumulate more expensive amenities to attract price-insensitive customers, students will continue to borrow more money to cover the tuition increases, and tuition prices will spiral ever higher.

Because of the moral hazard involved in the current system, economists like me are adamant that there needs to be a different approach to financing higher education to reverse perpetually growing tuition costs.

Taking the government out of financial aid is the solution I would propose to reduce college prices. This action would pull large amounts of easy credit out of the student loan industry and force lenders to scrutinize each college loan application. Banks would not issue loans to students that they believe could not pay them back. Therefore, students wouldn't have the ability to take on massive debt loads to enroll in programs that will result in low paying jobs after school. In a world without all these subsidies and government-guaranteed loans, the way people would pay for higher education is more or less the same way they pay for it now:

-Students are going to pay out of their own pockets for what they can afford.

-Students will then borrow money to cover any remaining balances.

The fundamental difference is that colleges would have to significantly cut their expenses to bring down the price of tuition because their customers wouldn't be flush with borrowed cash to pay for their overpriced degree programs.

<u>To sum up the college subsidy problem using economic jargon:</u>

The *moral hazard* created by government-supported financing for higher education leads to a system of extremely *inelastic demand (i.e., consumers don't change their purchasing habits for a product despite price increases/decreases)* for college degrees. Consumers (students) are making reckless decisions with the borrowed cash that they're provided with to finance their purchase (higher education). Suppliers (colleges) have no incentive to keep their prices low since they know that demand is extremely inelastic for their products. Politicians are incentivized to vote to increase the subsidy year after year because the beneficiaries of the financing are more vocal than the taxpayers who are paying to subsidize these loans. For the politician, it's a classic problem of concentrated benefits and diffused costs.

Topic 26: Are you saying that poor students shouldn't be able to receive financing for certain degrees?

For those concerned with equity— I can't see anything fairer than having a free market system in education. This system would result in wealthy parents wasting their money to pay for their kids to fail in the job market if they choose to study subjects like art and philosophy. Meanwhile, poor students would be restricted to study subjects that lenders would finance based on the likelihood that the student will be able to earn an income that is high enough to support themselves and pay off their student loans.

This system would discourage poor students from making *poor* choices (pun intended).

Topic 27: Didn't free markets and greed cause the economic collapse in 2008?

Most people know that the catalyst of the 2008 economic crash was bad mortgages. Surprise Surprise, housing prices, and the overall economy collapses when trillions of dollars in home loans are at risk of default. What most people don't know is how the mortgage market was set up and why home loans were being given out to financially questionable borrowers in the first place. The usual explanation for what triggered the Great Recession is the usual one—blame a single red herring. In this case, most people accused the banks of wrongdoing. *Greedy mortgage lenders gave out loans that they knew borrowers couldn't pay back. The investment banks then overexposed themselves to securities related to bundled mortgages (Traditional Residential Mortgage Backed Security or **TRMBS** for short). Finally, the investment banks made further profits off of the risk from their secondary mortgage market investments by trading Credit Default Swaps (insurance policies used to protect holders of debt* *from default) related to mortgage debt.* That is all true, mortgage lenders and investment banks did all of the above to create the malinvestment that screwed up the economy, but that is only a partial telling of the story. Anyone who has ever lent or borrowed money should have a few questions about the above explanation of what caused the great recession. The most obvious question is, "Why would mortgage lenders loan out money to borrowers who couldn't pay them back?" Would you let a stranger borrow $50, knowing that he would tell you to, "Get lost I'm broke," when you returned to collect?

To understand how the housing crash was a deviation from free-market principles and is tied to the activities of our "compassionate politicians," we have to introduce two entities— Fannie Mae and Freddie Mac. These two organizations were established to make mortgages more accessible to the public. Fannie and Freddie did this by purchasing the mortgages from home lenders and creating a *securitized debt* product *(e.g., TRMBS).* In this case, securitized debt is a term used to describe debt that has been sold by the original lender to an investor looking to make money off of the future payments made by the borrower. The buying & selling of these TRMBS securities is known as the *Secondary Mortgage Market.*

The mortgage market that was set up by Fannie and Freddie worked like this:

1. A borrower is given a mortgage loan by their lender to purchase a house.

2. The lender would then sell these mortgages to Fannie and Freddie. The lenders continued to service the debt, which means that the mortgage company collected the borrower's payments.

3. The mortgages were then packaged together (securitized) into a TRMBS based on how risky the loans were (e.g., credit scores of the borrowers, income, down payment, etc.).

4. Fannie and Freddie then went out to find investors to purchase these TRMBS securities in the secondary mortgage market.

5. Finally, the monthly mortgage payments made by the borrowers of the home loans were used to pay the investors who bought the TRMBS securities.

It's pretty clear why everybody played their part in this whole operation and why it all looks great on the surface.

The mortgage companies—sell the mortgages to Fannie and Freddie because they get paid back immediately on the principal of the loans they issued, plus a little bit of the future interest payments from the borrowers, without having to wait 15-30 years for the homeowner to pay them back. This system allows lenders to issue more mortgages since

Fannie and Freddie are limiting the amount of time they need to put up their own money when making loans.

Fannie and Freddie—are buying and bundling the mortgages into TRMBS investments because they're *Government Sponsored Enterprises* (GSE's) tasked with expanding homeownership by providing liquidity to the lenders (i.e., the money to make the loans).

Investors—are purchasing the TRMBS securities because they want an investment product with a "safe" and steady return. Their profit is the interest being paid by the homeowner, minus the premium paid to the lenders to purchase the mortgage.

Citizens—support this because it makes it easier for them to get mortgages to buy houses since lenders are more inclined to issue loans with the help of the GSE's.

Politicians—are pushing this whole system because they get credit from their constituents for making it easier to buy a home.

Look at this model long enough, and the inherent flaws become apparent.

The mortgage companies—don't care about who they issue mortgages to, since the second they make a loan for a home, Fannie and Freddie step in to buy the mortgage from them. Therefore, unqualified borrowers who would probably have extreme difficulty making the monthly payments on their home loans will still get their mortgage applications approved by these companies. The lenders don't face market consequences (e.g., never getting paid back) for issuing these loans since Fannie and Freddie purchase them almost immediately after the borrowers close on their house.

Fannie and Freddie—don't care about losing money because they are seemingly backed by the government.

Investors and Credit Rating Agencies—do not think twice about the possibility that these debt instruments will lose money, as it's seemingly issued by the government through the GSE's. Everybody fully expected the government to step in if these securities ever showed any signs of failing.

Citizens—believe they can afford to pay higher prices for their houses than their financial situation would realistically allow since most lenders are approving their loan applications. These borrowers experience little or no pushback on their income or ability to produce a healthy down payment. This system creates a higher risk of default because people borrow more money than they should. Also, housing prices become inflated because borrowers have easier access to loans, allowing them to offer higher bids to secure the houses they want to purchase.

In the end, if anything went wrong, every participant (except for the homebuyers) in this system *correctly* assumed that the government would bail them out.

Thankfully, the politicians and their bureaucrats who initially implemented this system were smart enough to see this moral hazard and recognized that borrowers and lenders would act recklessly if the risk of mortgage defaults were transferred from the initial lender to a third party. To reduce the moral hazard, the government limited the kind of mortgages that Fannie and Freddie could buy by setting loan standards, so only people with a good credit history qualified. Now, what's the problem with creating a program that only helps people with good credit buy houses, you might ask? By doing that, the government is just crafting a plan to help well-off Americans finance their homes, as those with higher credit rating scores tend to be wealthier. Also, housing prices will still become inflated from the easy credit being extended to the middle class. Unfortunately, over time the government program did what all government programs do—it expanded to cover more people. Fannie and Freddie ended up buying and securitizing riskier loans.

If you take Fannie and Freddie out of the equation, a recession caused by increasing mortgage defaults and artificially inflated housing prices would have been less severe or never happened. Why? The market for mortgage securitization wouldn't have been as large because investors and credit rating agencies would have assessed mortgage defaults accurately instead of relying on the implicit guarantee of a government bailout if homeowners stopped making their mortgage payments. As a result of a small market for mortgage securitization, mortgage lenders would have to keep more of the loans they made instead of having the ability to sell them to third parties. Since the lenders would hold onto the risk associated with the debt they issued, they would: decline the mortgage applications that contained borrowers with bad credit histories; reject applicants with a no/small down payment to put towards a house;

scrutinize the actions of their loan officers; and limit the size/amount of home loans that they issued. Therefore, people with bad credit would have never gotten approved for mortgage loans that they couldn't pay back in the first place, and qualified borrowers wouldn't have received staggering loans to bid up home prices. To sum it up, without government assistance, lenders would have to put up their own money if a borrower defaulted on a loan so that they wouldn't make loans lightly.

The argument, "The banks messed up and blew up the economy," is prevalent because it's a simple slogan that anybody can repeat. And it feels good to have an already maligned group (bankers) to blame for all of the calamity caused by a well-intentioned policy. Any accurate explanation of the causal events that led up to the Great Recession will be multifaceted (my analysis barely scratched the surface of the messy mortgage market) and require a good deal of knowledge on how the financial system for mortgage loans operates. In other words: the economic reality of a recession caused by malinvestment from the moral hazard set up by bad public policy can't compete with the tale being told about greedy banks and helpless homeowners. Are banks to blame for the mortgage meltdown? Absolutely. But also responsible are the: politicians that ordered the GSE's to expand the secondary mortgage market; the borrowers that took out loans that they couldn't afford to pay back; the credit rating agencies that rated the debt based on the implicit guarantee of the government; and the investors that expected the government to bail them out if people stopped paying back their mortgages. In a situation where there are no real victims, you have to look at what enables this broken system to operate. In this case, the issue was the secondary mortgage market that Fannie and Freddie were pumping up at the government's command.

<u>Conclusion</u>

Politicians and the public have consistently made the mistake of believing that their compassion and goodwill will allow them to create economic policies that can benefit the poor and middle-class while transferring all of the negative consequences to the rich. Economists know from thoroughly examining these policies that this alchemy has not yet been achieved. The actions that are taken to help the poor and middle class by our benevolent leaders, in response to the demands of their well-meaning citizens, have instead: cheated unskilled workers and welfare beneficiaries out of opportunities to accumulate skills; prevented government aid recipients from saving money to improve their futures; and enabled college students and homebuyers to make terrible financial decisions. I hope that this book has reinforced the importance of critical thinking when it comes to critiquing the popular narratives surrounding economic issues. In this book, I outlined the cause and effect outcomes that economists have long talked about when presenting arguments about why it does not help the poor to put in place: the minimum wage, welfare programs, anti-profit policies, and subsidies.

- *If you make something more expensive, people will buy less of it.* Therefore, raising the price employers have to pay their unskilled workers via minimum wage mandates will always increase the unemployment rate among low-skilled workers. In the long run, this stunts the ability of workers on the bottom rungs of the job market from acquiring the skills to raise their income potential.

- *People will always try to maximize the benefits they receive and minimize the costs that they pay.* In many cases, welfare provides unemployed recipients equivalent net value through government benefits than a low-skilled worker would receive by working. And so, a large number of unskilled workers will choose to receive taxpayer-funded resources over the option of taking a low-paying job. Therefore, these programs are inadvertently bribing unskilled workers to avoid pursuing opportunities to develop skills in low paying jobs. These skills are the prerequisites to landing higher-paying positions in the future.

- *When you limit the ability of individuals and businesses to keep the profits they earn, they'll have less of an incentive to work hard and invest in capital.* It should be self-evident why the economy would suffer when you remove the incentive from workers to work hard. Regarding capital investment, the productivity rate of workers dramatically shrinks when businesses stop investing in capital because workers will have less access to the equipment that enables them to perform their jobs effectively. Both scenarios result in less stuff being produced for consumers.

- *When you subsidize people to engage in risky behaviors by lowering their present costs (moral hazard), they'll be more likely to engage in counterproductive activities that have severe long term consequences.* Since the government subsidizes the costs associated with higher education, students that are not prepared to study a major with a viable career path are lured into wasting precious time and money to attend college to get a degree with little or no practical application. According to the same logic: when politicians insure banks against the risk of losing money on mortgage loans (via the creation of GSE's that securitize and insure mortgage loans); they will give out loans to applicants with poor credit histories; and borrowers who have a high chance of defaulting on their mortgage payments.

There are no easy answers to the questions surrounding how a society can quickly lift people out of poverty and reduce inequality. This is one of the reasons why Economics is known as *"The Dismal Science."* Economists don't have any nice-sounding solutions, and most of our findings and policy recommendations appear cold and cruel on the surface. The conclusion most economists have come up with to alleviate poverty and improve outcomes for the poor and middle class are: allow low-skilled workers and businesses to set their own prices so that more unskilled workers can find jobs; do not disincentivize work with short-term benefits that lead to long-term poverty traps; do not restrict profit so that producers will continue to work hard and invest in the capital that brings down the prices for their customers, and not to subsidize decisions so that people are actively thinking about the consequences their choices have on their own futures. These conclusions do not appeal to the masses, who are demanding answers on how a society can quickly reach utopian levels of prosperity with no tradeoffs.

The smartest message an economist can deliver to their friends and family on the topic of economics is silence. Any conversation about the subject will end badly for the person basing their arguments on logical conclusions.

Appendix

1. "Characteristics of minimum wage workers, 2015: BLS Reports." U.S. Bureau of Labor Statistics. April 2016. Accessed August 29, 2016. https://www.bls.gov/opub/reports/minimum-wage/2015/home.htm.

2. "Labor Force Statistics from the Current Population Survey." U.S. Bureau of Labor Statistics. October 2015. Accessed August 29, 2016. https://www.bls.gov/opub/reports/minimum-wage/2015/home.htm.

3. Costco Wholesale Corporation (2015). 10-K Annual Report 2015. Accessed August 29, 2016, from SEC EDGAR website.

4. "QuickFacts." U.S. Census Bureau QuickFacts selected: UNITED STATES. Accessed August 29, 2016. https://www.census.gov/quickfacts/fact/table/US/PST045216.

5. DeHaven, Tad. "Corporate Welfare in the Federal Budget." Cato Institute. July 25, 2012. Accessed August 29, 2016. https://www.cato.org/publications/policy-analysis/corporate-welfare-federal-budget.

6. "Policy Basics: Introduction to Medicaid." Center on Budget and Policy Priorities. August 16, 2016. Accessed August 29, 2016. https://www.cbpp.org/research/health/policy-basics-introduction-to-medicaid.

7. "The Conference Board Total Economy Database™." The Conference Board. May 2017. Accessed August 29, 2016.

https://www.conference-board.org/data/economydatabase/index.cfm?id=27762.

8. EXXON MOBIL CORPORATION (2015). 10-K Annual Report 2015. Accessed August 29, 2016, from SEC EDGAR website.

9. "Median Household Income in the Past 12 Months (in 2015 inflation-adjusted dollars)". American Community Survey. United States Census Bureau. 2015. Archived from the original on 17 April 2016. Accessed August 29, 2016.

10. Employment Policies Institute. (2017). *Employment Policies Institute | Minimum Wage: Teen Unemployment*. [online] Available at: https://www.epionline.org/minimum-wage/minimum-wage-teen-unemployment/ [Accessed 21 Sep. 2017].

11. "Entry-Level Graphic Artist Salary." Entry Level Graphic Artist Salary. September 16, 2017. Accessed September 22, 2017.
https://www.payscale.com/research/US/Job=Graphic_Artist/Hourly_Rate/ebe62ac2/Entry-Level.

12. "Entry-Level Software Engineer Salary." Entry Level Software Engineer Salary. September 20, 2017. Accessed September 22, 2017.
https://www.payscale.com/research/US/Job=Software_Engineer/Salary/4fd947de/Entry-Level.

13. "Tuition Inflation." Tuition Inflation. July 02, 2019. Accessed July 05, 2019. http://www.finaid.org/savings/tuition-inflation.phtml.

www.ingramcontent.com/pod-product-compliance
Lightning Source LLC
Chambersburg PA
CBHW022037190326
41520CB00008B/619